THE 1865
STONEMAN'S
RAID BEGINS

THE 1865 STONEMAN'S RAID BEGINS

Leave Nothing for the Rebellion to Stand Upon

JOSHUA BEAU BLACKWELL

THE
History
PRESS

Published by The History Press
Charleston, SC 29403
www.historypress.net

First published 2011

ISBN 9781540234780

Library of Congress Cataloging-in-Publication Data

Blackwell, Joshua Beau.
The 1865 Stoneman Raid begins : leave nothing for the rebellion to stand upon / Joshua
Beau Blackwell.
p. cm.
Includes bibliographical references and index.
ISBN 978-1-59629-849-1
1. Stoneman's Raid, 1865. 2. Stoneman, George, 1822-1894. I. Title.
E477.9.B55 2011
973.7'38--dc22
2011008306

To my favorite person:
please forgive me for my countless faults…

Contents

Preface

Early in June 2009, I found myself trapped in a classroom full of semiconscious educators who had been begrudgingly coaxed into sacrificing a week of their lives in order to attend a seminar at the University of Georgia. As my eyelids began to increase in weight, it dawned on me that the worm had definitely turned. In the current milieu of educational theory, which unequivocally holds that the optimal way to raise student test scores is by encouraging engaging and explorative learning, I thought to myself, what better way to encourage student interest than to bore the hell out of their instructors? Until that point, the highlight of the seminar on instructional methods in European history had been a few embarrassingly offhanded remarks toward the instructor offered in a vain effort to maintain what little remained of my sanity. At the moment of truth between slumber and apathetic boredom, the tone of my cellphone disturbed the slumber of many of my fellow professional development inmates. Initially ignoring the chiming phone, I let my digital leash transition over to voicemail.

In the midst of inhaling a well-deserved breath of fresh air and conversing with a teacher from Lincolnton, North Carolina, regarding the wasted merits of this week of our lives that was lost forever, I finally dialed my voicemail. The message was, needless to say, unexpected. Returning the call, the individual who answered the other end of the line was a man by the name of Doug Bostick, who was freelancing as a series editor for The History Press. After exchanging a few pleasantries, we arrived at the heart of the matter.

The publisher was producing a series of works that would pay homage to many of the minor campaigns and incidents of the American Civil War.

Inquiring as to how I fit into the picture, Doug informed me that my name and number had been dropped to him by the staff of the South Carolina Relic Room as a historian who would be interested in penning a commission piece centering on a campaign conducted in Appalachia during the war. With my professional academic interest grounded in cultural conflicts within Appalachia, I was intrigued to hear that he was looking for someone to write a modern narrative on the largest campaign to affect the Southern Appalachians during the conflict: the Stoneman Raid of 1865.

After further discussion, I became interested in the proposal due to the challenges and narrative possibilities that it offered. The first item to grab my attention was the timetable—a delivery date that fell within the winter of 2010–11. With preproduction scheduled for under eighteen months, and the fact that I had yet to conduct a stitch of research, the opportunity to test my archival mettle was certainly appealing. The condition that sealed the deal, however, was an understanding that the work was not to be academic. Constantly in search of a challenge, I was chomping at the bit to produce a work of popular history, since my first work, "*Used to Be a Rough Place in Them Hills": Moonshine, the Dark Corner, and the New South*, had satisfied my immediate urge to contribute to the historiography of the South.

The end result of the following year's labor was a piece that I never anticipated writing, as I have always viewed American Civil War military history as an intriguing, but heavily saturated, historical topic. Though set against the backdrop of a well-studied time period, the Stoneman Raid has avoided developing the bloated library of academic works, narrative publications and historical fiction that many of its counterparts possess. The absence of myriad publications on the subject has given me the opportunity to bring to light a handful of personal accounts, which were previously ignored or relegated to footnotes, for the present generation. Furthermore, as a firm believer in the merits of narrative history and oral tradition, only a cursory glance at any local library that stands along the paths the raiders took unveils a mammoth collection of recorded stories concerning both raider debauchery and civilian hardship. With such a large collection of stories, this book has given me the opportunity to engage in a style that I have long hoped to experiment with—the employment of the narrative license that microhistory offers in order to explore a larger topic of study.

Fingerville, South Carolina
December 2010

Acknowledgements

As a student of history, I have cultivated a strong interest in the unsung struggles of the lower class from Southern Appalachia and the endless barricades that have confronted them. Whether it be aggressive revenue enforcement following the end of the American Civil War, the encroachment of outsiders into the region or economic exploitation of natural resources, the impoverished inhabitants of Appalachia, like countless other cultural enclaves throughout the United States, have been subjected to a multitude of hardships at the hands of their supposed social betters. The nature of this work is not to address these issues directly, but to provide informative entertainment for those who wish to develop a greater appreciation for the tragedy that was the War Between the States in the mountain South. Although it goes without saying that my deep appreciation for those who push back against the impositions of the social elite is present in the undertones of the following pages, their story is to be told at another point in time.

Through the journey of this work, much undue stress has been put on relationships that mean the world to me. Although fleeting words can do little to repair the rift that two years of negligent labor can carve, hopefully the gratitude that I hold will serve as the first steps in easing the pain that I have caused many. Although pardon after pardon should be asked of my family for the reclusive behavior I have demonstrated over the past year, one recent addition to my life is owed a deep apology for lack of return in her emotional investments. I am sorry, and you, above all others, are responsible for my last threads of sanity.

ACKNOWLEDGEMENTS

As with any form of expression that requires the help of others, I have thought long and hard to compile an adequate list of those who deserve recognition for their role in the construction of this book. First, thanks must be extended to Doug Bostick and The History Press for enlisting my help to recount a story that has fascinated me since I was young. Their grace and patience throughout this process have been unmatched by my experiences with other publishers. Second, I would like to thank Barbara Gehlmann and Beverly Pournelle for their assistance in preparing the manuscript. Agreeing to edit the final draft, without recompense, has salvaged any opportunity to maintain the timetable suggested by The History Press.

Finally, I find myself shouldering a major debt of gratitude toward my dearest friend and emotional punching bag, Sarah Caldwell. The amount of time she has devoted to molding this script has been essential to the publication ever seeing the light of day. It will be to my everlasting regret that all the kind attention and understanding she has shown me was, at best, apathetically returned. Once again, I can unequivocally proclaim that without the labor press-ganged out of her, little of my efforts would be worth the cost of ink.

Introduction

Stoneman's Carolina Raid

There is only a finite dose of pain that can be administered to the human body before the senses collectively melt in agony. Once this sensual threshold is crossed, the mind delivers a queer sensation, one where the agonizing signals to the brain transform into a visual spectacle for the mind. In this aesthetic, a bright flash originating within the deepest recesses of the mind takes center stage, the illuminated manifestation of the mind abandoning the body to its fate. This illusion, facilitated by the flat end of a square-tipped shovel thrust across the lower back, welcomed Dr. Henry Winthrop back into the world.

It took just a few moments for the weathered physician to assess the gravity of his situation. His hands were bound, a roughly constructed noose bit into the bottom of his Adam's apple and excruciating pain raced through his torso as he served as the focal point in a room full of strangers, who were impatiently inspecting their victim for any sign of capitulation, their universally lustful stare dancing between fanaticism and utter greed. Such was the milieu in the master bedroom of the home of Dr. Henry Ravenel on May 2, 1865.[1]

It was a scene of panoramic chaos. The oak bedstead, and its unfortunate association with the hemp rope that was secured intimately around the neck of the good doctor, creaked under the stress of every breath and hard-fought swallow. Muddy, ragged and hungover, the strangers who filled the room were intoxicated beyond all repair by greed. This coupling of outlaws was chiefly driven by the horrifying realization that this particular Tuesday morning was most likely their final opportunity to share in the spoils of war. Among the distinguishing elements that separated these lustful scoundrels from the thousands of young men who had passed through Pendleton, South Carolina, during the preceding four years of war were the damnable contraptions cockily clutched in their dominant hands, vacillating from side to side like doll-babies swung by inattentive children—the seven-shot Spencer repeating carbine.[2]

However, the worst was far from over, as a closefisted punch to the incapacitated doctor's left ear signaled that this agonizingly reflective intermission had come to a swift end. "Where is it?" demanded a blurry image that was hoisting what appeared to be a shovel above his head. Doing his best not to concentrate on the fresh burning sensation pulsating from his wounded ear, Dr. Winthrop tried to process the request with lightning speed.[3]

Alas, there was no time. The next blow descended upon the victim like a meteor, striking across his rib cage and ultimately smashing against the right elbow. Yet again, the increasingly familiar flash engulfed his field of vision. This time, it was accompanied by a gagging sensation that seemed to drive his entire throat into a compacted knot below a surprised set of tonsils, leaving the doctor with a queasy sensation in his stomach that was unmatched by any injury he had experienced in his previous sixty-two years. It was at that moment that the realization of what was actually happening to him came crashing down on his consciousness with the weight of the world: "I'm being hanged with the tips of my dammed toes touching the floor."[4]

The sobering blow of an uppercut to the breadbasket focused the wavering attention of the doctor solely on his interrogator. Staring cross-eyed at the shadowy figure, the befuddling words echoed through his ears, "Damn your eyes, where did you hide the gold?" As the shadow raised his hands for another assault, the unseen inquisitor continued, "I swear to God I will jesse your ass right here and now!" Trying to find both words and air enough in his diaphragm to answer the assailant's misguided questions, the only audible sounds produced by Dr. Winthrop were gurgling hacks augmented by a small murmur.[5]

The man striking the ancient doctor was a member of Major General George Stoneman's East Tennessee Cavalry Division of the United States Army, which on that day fell under a confusing proxy command structure that had all but collapsed. The focus of this soldier's lust was a deposit of gold rumored to be squirreled away within the estate. While silverware, luxury items and gold currency had been the darlings of the troopers' attention since their descent into South Carolina via Jones Gap, the ultimate treasure-trove that drove the men into frenzy was the entire Confederate treasury. The store of Rebel bullion was rumored to be hidden in the area, just as the same fortune was whispered to be buried in the cellar of every mansion within the upstate of South Carolina. By early May 1865, this quickly developing legend was probable cause enough for a government-sanctioned home invasion.[6]

Of the stimulations that inundated the old man's senses, one trumped all: the desperate pleas of his niece, Caroline Ravenel, who beseeched the raiders to cease their inhuman activity. Every blow thrust upon her battered uncle only served to intensify the squeals for mercy from the young woman. "What are you talking about?" meekly cried the socialite. In a whimpering burst of exhalation, she pleaded, "Please, for the love of God, stop this madness!" Naturally, it was her adamant stance that the rumors of gold on the property were, in fact, just that.[7]

The only response to the pleas of the maiden was a pair of quick jabs across the face of the old doctor. These bursts of frustration were, of course, an indication that the trooper had lost his patience with the inquisition. "Cut the son-of-a-bitch down," bellowed the long-drawn Appalachian accent of the interrogator, "he ain't talking—yet." Instantaneously, a trooper stepped on the mattress of the bed with his hand in the pocket of his prominent leg, produced and unfolded his pocketknife and took a couple of repetitious slashes at the rope just below the bedstead. As the trooper butchered the intertwined hemp, the rope began to unravel and finally gave way. A sharp snap sent the doctor plummeting face first to the floor with a hollow thud. As his nose and teeth were greeted by the pine floorboards, the victim found himself freed from his deadly conundrum.[8]

No sooner had Winthrop fallen to the floor than two cavalrymen grabbed him by his bound arms and dragged him out of the room. Brushing Ms. Ravenel out of their way as she desperately reached for her uncle, the troopers bypassed the socialite, and the trio staggered down the hallway toward the staircase. At the top of the stairs, the trooper who stood to the left of the doctor slid his right leg between the victim's feet as the offender handling Winthrop's right hemisphere thrust his victim forward. Following an earth-shattering tumble down the stairs, Henry was brought back to his senses by a trooper kicking him in an effort to roll him over on his back. After the limp old man was sprawled squarely on his back, a trooper grabbed the doctor by his lapels and lifted the battered physician to his feet.[9]

"Tell me damn it!" was the only warning the doctor had before his face was driven through a plaster wall. The natural results of this action were several lacerations across the face, a broken nose and a notable deviation from the premeditated interrogation that the doctor had faced just a few moments before—a clear sign that desperation had consumed the cavalrymen. As the battered man slumped down the shattered wall, his eyes clearly revealed that the will to fight was gone and that his interrogators had successfully worked him over.

Unable to fully open his eyes, a peculiar sensation at the back of his neck alerted him to the seriousness of the situation. His senses came rushing back to him as the presence of the cold barrel of a Remington revolver kissed the stiff hair that had arisen just south of his brainstem. The sound of three simple mechanical gears rotating a cylinder as the hammer was withdrawn from its home became all the indication the doctor needed to fully comprehend that if he did not pacify his interrogators, this hellish transaction would be his last experience in this world.[10]

"Stop it! Stop! Stop!" were the only cries flowing from Caroline as she tried to force herself down the staircase, which was now inhabited by the mess of troopers. One rider, obviously frustrated with the morning's developments, turned to her and chambered a round in his Spencer. "Listen here cockchafer," he said, the hollow tone of his voice only adding weight to the message, "if we don't get what we want from the old man, were going to string up you and your mother next!" The fact that the troopers were still aware that her mother was in the house, despite the lack of the unseen woman's witness to the interrogation, was all that was needed to silence Caroline. As the shock of being directly threatened for the first time in her life crept over her, all the lady could do was emote inaudible murmurs of sheer hate. It was a feeling Ms. Ravenel never forgot and one on which she publicly reflected with haunting regularity for the remainder of her life.[11]

Fully understanding that his interrogators had every intention of ending his existence, Dr. Winthrop whimpered the most heart-wrenching words that his mouth had ever uttered: "The chimney, it's stowed away in the chimney." No sooner had the verbal betrayal traversed his lips than regret saturated his body, exploding a criticism that was malevolently generated by his conscience and tore through an already weakened mind. Collapsing introspectively, the doctor lamented, "You blaspheming weakling, you bastard, how dare you give them exactly what they wanted!"[12]

Lifting the old man to his feet, the troopers began to incessantly badger their victim with a fresh barrage of inquiries. In an effort to pacify a flood of new questions, the information was freely given up without corporal encouragement. While Caroline was allowed to descend the stairs and tend to her shattered uncle, the troopers practically trampled her as they swarmed the upper levels of the house. Moments later, as a soot-encrusted bundle was retrieved from behind the mantel of a chamber fireplace on the second floor, elation filled the room. However, fate quickly quelled their joy as the troopers came to the realization that their morning efforts had all been in vain, and a portion of the purloined Confederate treasury had not been discovered. Instead, all that was liberated from the cradle of secession were the last few gold dollars of a previously wealthy, yet currently bankrupt, family.[13]

This scene of quasi-sanctioned governmental terrorism, eagerly dismissed as the call of duty, was enacted in the twilight hours of one of the most epic struggles in the annals of the English-speaking world. The alcohol-inspired debauchery by representatives of the United States Army was undertaken nearly half a week after Joseph Eggleston Johnston surrendered to William Tecumseh Sherman at the Bennett homestead in North Carolina, an event that should have brought the conflict east of the Blue Ridge to a close. Furthermore, the affront occurred in the face of many veterans of the Army of Northern Virginia a full three weeks after Robert E. Lee surrendered at Appomattox Court House and functionally ended the war in the minds of all but the most devoted secessionists.

The Stoneman Raid into the Carolinas, with side ventures into Virginia and Georgia, was the most important auxiliary operation of the entire conflict, in spite of the handicap of its late inauguration. Departing Knoxville, Tennessee, with three planned objectives in late March 1865, the raid transformed in definition and scope almost daily. Originally designed as a demoralizing strike against the few remaining operational rail lines in the region, by the middle of May, the raid had transformed into a multifaceted operation that ultimately aided in forcing the surrender of two major Confederate armies, rendered hundreds of miles of track useless east of the mountains, destroyed a major Confederate prison, incinerated many of the remaining major military resources of the Southern nation, terrorized the civilian populations in its path and drove the fugitive Confederate presidential cat into the bag. Needless to say, the raid quickly became one of the longest and most taxing cavalry operations of the entire war.

Furthermore, it was the last act in a series of devastating campaigns that wore the mantle of the new nomenclature of total war. While seemingly critical to the later war effort, the major detraction of the campaign was that this military experiment was conducted on a civilian population largely unaffected by the war and residing in a region of little strategic importance to the ultimate outcome of the conflict. Moreover, with the bulk of the war behind them, the raid amounted to little more than adding insult to injury—a well-calculated message to the unaffected communities of the Confederacy that their defeat was total and universally shared.

In spite of its tactical success, the raid was ultimately a tragic waste of resources for both sides. Almost entirely channeled toward civilian populations, property and psyche, the campaign has lived on well past the cessation of hostilities, leaving a lasting impression on the local folklore of the Appalachian, foothill and piedmont realms of four states. Local folklore spawned numerous tales concerning the conduct of the raiders. Although most are grounded in exaggerated truth, the gravity of the raid also lent itself to the wilds of the imagination, encouraging the fabrication of colorful falsities that are still widely recorded.

However, the raid was also a testament to the efficiency of the United States Army and the pinnacle example of what cavalry was capable of in modern warfare. Striking out of Knoxville, Tennessee, on March 21 with approximately six thousand well-equipped troopers, one wagon, four cannons and ten ambulances, the raiders covered an unprecedented amount of terrain and fought skirmishes at breakneck speed. Almost as soon as the raid had begun, Stoneman saw it to his advantage to sever all ties with his base of supply by abandoning the cumbersome ambulances and returning the heavy fieldpieces to Knoxville. Continuing the path outlined for the raid by utilizing the countryside, civilian property and military stores as his provender, Stoneman imposed on the inhabitants of the upland South the same hardships witnessed in areas such as central Georgia.

The astounding mastery of the logistics employed to move six thousand mounted men across hundreds of miles of hostile territory was unmatched. Most remarkable of the logistical accomplishments was maintaining the adequate number of commandeered mounts needed to keep up with the lightning pace of the raid. The swift completion of the plethora of objectives, many rising without credence or previous intelligence, and the infliction of catastrophic damage upon the enemy with only minimal loss, is telling of the determination of the men who undertook the raid.[14]

Aside from the astonishing logistical mastery of the raid and the lesson that it provides students of military history, the entire campaign was also a story—the narrative of personal experience. The raid can be viewed as the vindication of the disgraced father of modern cavalry operations, who salvaged his reputation from obscurity. It is also the story of revenge garnered by rustic individuals who had spent their entire existence outside the antebellum mainstream and constantly under the scornful scrutiny of the cotton aristocracy. To these outsiders, the war became a question of personal and family allegiance. Finally, it was the most fulfilling and financially rewarding adventure that many supporters of the Union would experience in their entire wartime careers—a fitting conclusion to four hellish years of heartbreaking slaughter.

It is undeniable that the raid affected the civilian populace of the various regions it traversed more so than perhaps any other single event of the nineteenth century. With this fact in mind, the following work sets out to achieve a comprehensive study of the raid through the intimate interweaving of recorded history with the cultural folklore that the campaign produced. Not only will the actions and consequences of the raiders be evaluated, but also the memories—whether truth, exaggeration or outright fabrication—will be presented alongside the historical record, as it is my opinion that when an event affects culture to the magnitude of this raid, folklore and history became one and the same.

Finally, this work will address a long-neglected aspect concerning the history of the raid: interclass warfare. Although the actions of the Appalachian troopers have been vilified in the past, it is my opinion that the raid offered the lower classes of Appalachia, from Kentucky to Western North Carolina, an outlet to assault the upper-class interest of their region. From participants in what were then known as "Home Yankee" regiments to their civilian camp followers and renegade blacks from the mountains, the lower class exerted much of its antebellum frustrations on its supposed social betters during the campaign. The culminating result of the raid was that its actions became ingrained in the cultural fabric of the outlying regions of the Confederacy for the next generation.[15]

1

"Than to Be Amongst Those Who Owe Their Escape to Considerations of Self-Preservation"

"Goddamn Southern sun, goddamn Tejana dust, goddamn infernal heat, goddamn this lousy mount, goddamn my bloody shredded hide, goddamn that traitorous Twiggs, goddamn secessionist, goddamn rebellion, goddamn my whole miserable existence!" Incessant repetition, the hallmark of an embittered internal monologue, raced through the middle-aged captain's mind. "So, this is where life has taken me, running for my hide through damnation from those traitorous bastards." He cast a bloodshot eye at the long, earth-shrouded column as the brooding continued, "Leading mongoloids who could not pour piss out of a boot if the damned directions were written on the heel." As the miles passed, the mental grievances only multiplied as the sun broiled down on the dusty column of troopers, mounted infantry, nervous civilians and countless wagons filled with government property.

The enormity of the situation bore its full effect on the psyche of the column's helmsman, as the signature scowl consumed his long face and mangled beard. The deeply hollow stare and grimace intertwined with his other physical features so perfectly that they seemed to become one and the same with his personality. The fire that engulfed his battered ego generated an uneasy glint in his eyes, giving the appearance that the captain was either on the border of collapsing into madness or into a fit of rage. This painfully silent disposition had an unexpectedly comforting effect on the morale of his retreating troopers. The ice-cold stare of the rider was a constant trait that his men had come to expect, and the facial expression borne by their leader was a sure indication that no matter how badly their situation deteriorated, some facts remained the same—Captain Stoneman was still pissed off at everything.

Unbeknownst to his makeshift cavalcade—comprising veteran cavalrymen born in the North; aging, Southern-born noncommissioned officers who could not bear to turn against their flag; rookie officers with their hearts in the right place; bloated quartermasters; and sympathetic civilians—his brooding temper flared to the depths of his soul. Nearly one thousand miles from friendly territory, the renegade commander feared the worst if the Texans closed the distance. On the verge of breaking down under the stress piled high on his shoulders, rivaling the weight bestowed upon Atlas by Hercules, he looked for any semblance of calming tranquility within. None was found. "God damn my putrid life!"[16]

As the column pressed on, the miles metamorphosed into hours, the hours amassed into days and the days melded into an eternity. "Is this a fool's errand?" he thought as the terror of looming and unforeseen consequences began to take root in his mind. "Are we headed toward a trap?" As the paranoia that can only be generated by fatal mistakes sprouted, the officer's mind began to spin into panic. "Is the port already in rebel hands; and if so, will those heartless Texans hang me for not heading to that damn trap in San Antonio?" His mind raced as the rogue band followed the slow, brackish water of the Rio Grande. Despite the angst that burned within the sufferer's body, he knew two facts to remain true: if he made it to safety, he would fight this rebellion with every ounce of energy his body could muster; and if he ever saw General David Twiggs again, the meeting would be infamously abrupt due to a well-placed round from his service revolver.[17]

The first instance where encouragement was allowed to puncture the inner sanctum of his heart was when the nostrils of the riders were tickled with the delightfully stagnant aroma of brackish river water, leading the entire ensemble to muse that just maybe this gamble would pay off. Rounding the final bend of the Rio Grande and looking across the barrier islands toward Brazos Santiago, one sight in particular signified that the effort had not been undertaken in vain: the old flag flying atop the post office. For the first time in his short career, the wayward New Yorker had taken his fate, and that of his men, into his own hands, and the fruits had been rewarding. The tension immediately left his body, a rare smile crossed his bearded face and his fears leapt from his body with great exuberance. All was going according to plan;

he was on top of the world, and all would be fine. He was destined for home. It was a fitting end to his peacetime existence and that of his loyalist rabble.[18]

The man who would lead the most exhaustive raid of the war, an adventure that crossed the Smokey Mountains of Tennessee and ended far beyond the Blue Ridge of the Carolinas, was almost as unimposing as he was daunting. Standing well in excess of six feet, George Stoneman was a stoic individual of monumental stature who could be described by a plethora of qualifiers; however, magnetic was certainly not one of them. Riding high in the saddle, his erectly narrow torso and long limbs presented the illusion of an equestrian giant. But his meekly quiet and mild persona betrayed this grandiose illusion.

Upon further examination of the rider, even the dullest observer was confronted with the memorable sight of this statuesque man, exemplified by his hauntingly sunken face projecting all the sorrow of a bruised soul that had long grown accustomed to catastrophic failure. Depressed within this unfortunate face were dark, lethargic saucers, which were capable of intermittently radiating sweet emotions of love and friendship or, just as easily, seething with pure hate. The mouth, crowned with narrow pointed lips that peaked and recessed across the course of the orifice, was tactfully masked by a beard that sprouted to chest length. This often-unkempt choice in facial hair was a keen finishing touch to the grand spectacle that this cavalry commander projected, leaving the immediate observer to ponder whether this particular individual was half-mad, half-wild or an adequate compromise between the two.

Despite his aesthetic handicaps and their hallmarks—his inadequacies burned upon his conscience by the sting of a less-than-stellar military career—the subject's abilities instantly garnered the attention of all who met him; although by 1865, the list of those who had not witnessed his professional shortcomings, like his list of friends, was growing shorter by the day. This calm and collected academic, more than willing to propose or accept tasks beyond his realm of ability, was a favorite of his instructors even early in his career. Incessantly mindful of anything remotely resembling dereliction of duty, this administrative-minded officer was a natural candidate for the many adjunct positions that would have driven even a mild-blooded officer to insanity. A supply strategist of the highest order, the intellect of this man was highly respected in the peacetime army. Unfortunately, his silent personality, accompanied by unheralded outbursts of violent and explosive temper, could quickly alienate him from colleagues and subordinate officers. To do any description of George Stoneman justice, it would be wise to mention that his persona was best described as a perfect parallel to that of his West Point roommate and close friend Thomas J. Jackson, who was one of the most notoriously stoic eccentrics to ever grace the halls of the academy.[19]

George Stoneman was born on the western frontier of New York in a small lumber town near Lake Chautauqua, then known as Busti, on August 8, 1822. The oldest of eight surviving children born to George Stoneman Sr. and Catherine Chaney Aldrich Stoneman, the young Stoneman was ushered into the world by a prosperous frontier family, whose patriarch served the community by executing warrants as the local justice of the peace and made a lucrative living as the operator of a sawmill. This up-and-coming family, with its foundations in the upper echelons of frontier society, only served to advance its prestige in the new republic through the careers of its children. Most of the Stoneman clan went on to notable professions, such as lawyers, college professors, an African botanist, state senators and multi-state gubernatorial successes. Young George alone sought a career in service to his country, much to the dismay of his parents, who viewed the decision as a waste of his natural talents.[20]

By existing accounts, young Stoneman excelled as a student. His headmaster at the rural Jamestown Academy noted that Stoneman demonstrated academic talent in subjects that titillated his fancy. In particular, the young man was attracted to higher-level mathematics, a predisposition that blossomed due to his introspective personality and mindful attention to the artful symmetry of detail. After having the military bug securely embedded in his ear by a serial article written about the school, the eldest Stoneman child sought an appointment to the United States Military Academy following his eighteenth birthday. Although his family was deprived of the quintessential political connections needed to wangle an appointment, fortune would shine on the aspiring candidate in spite of the deficiency. Luckily for George Stoneman, the year in question—1842—was void of acceptable candidates from New York to join the largest class the academy had yet to enroll. Thus, the dark-horse applicant secured his appointment on May 9, after fleeting correspondence with then secretary of war Abe Bell.[21]

However, with the appointment to the Corps of Cadets secure, George Stoneman was unable to establish himself among the outstanding notables of the historic class in which he found himself enrolled—arguably due to his modest background from the outer reaches of New York State. At the Military Academy, Stoneman was noted as being a reserved student, coming nowhere near the meteors of personalities that were his classmates: George E. Pickett, George B. McClellan and A.P. Hill. Stoneman, instead, looked inward, becoming introspective and short-spoken. It was noted by a West Point contemporary that George Stoneman was a reserved student of "unobtrusive, meditative disposition, rather a thinker than talker." The same breath was directed toward his friend and junior-year roommate, Thomas Jackson. Both Stoneman and Jackson embodied the more reserved pillars of one of the most talented graduating classes in school history. Though he had been an astute student at the rural New York academy, where he was cultivated, the advanced academic rigors of West Point proved challenging for Stoneman, who finished thirty-third out of a class of sixty students in 1846. Surprisingly, the mind that was later noted for its obsession with details and numbers was unable to eke out a standing in the upper half of his graduating class.[22]

Following his completion of the rigors of West Point and the conveniently timed culmination of the American goading of its southern neighbor, cleverly masked as a territorial dispute with Mexico, George Stoneman received a commission as second lieutenant in Company G of the First United States Dragoons. Transfer to the West was a whirlwind, and within a few weeks of his christening, the young lieutenant found himself a resident of Fort Leavenworth, Kansas. It was there that the freshman officer was presented with a challenging assignment for a wet-behind-the-ears officer, training the notoriously rowdy First Missouri Mounted Volunteers. His successful navigation of the nerve-shattering frustration that came hand in hand with attempting to organize such overtly independent soldiers surely aided Stoneman in his dealings with the unkempt and incorrigible Southern-born elements of his later commands. After his first assignment, Stoneman set out with General Stephen Watts Kearney and others on June 5, 1846, with the intention of liberating California from the shackles of Mexican oppression.[23]

Although absent from the grand campaigns against the Mexican army, Stoneman's relegation to the backwater theaters of California and Utah left him with a rather colorful wartime experience. The young Stoneman's first field assignment was indeed unique for a West Point academic; he was assistant quartermaster for the mythical Mormon Battalion during their trek west to secure emigration routes during the late summer of 1846 through the early spring of 1847. The march provided Stoneman with a lifelong memento of his service in the last great antebellum adventure: the loss of a portion of his right thumb to a chain fire in the cylinder of his sidearm at the onset of a cattle stampede. In addition to the amputation of the upper portion of his most valuable digit from his dominant hand, the march also scarred the young officer's ego with the burden of watching his first grandiose scheme unravel right before his very eyes.[24]

The young lieutenant, faced with a mounting shortage of supplies and a seemingly endless multitude of miles ahead of the ill-fated expedition, convinced his commanders to allow him the license to float the last few precious supplies of the battalion down the Gila River as part of a desperate last-ditch effort to reduce the distance between the supply base and their line of march. This ambitious proposal established a disastrous precedent, as the first sign of a chronic problem that tormented the officer for the entirety of his career surfaced: magnificently inspired plans that manifested themselves horribly. The soggy disaster that ensued resulted in the unintentional scuttling of the majority of the battalion's supplies, a weeklong backtrack to recover any quantity of the waterlogged rations and a further reduction in the caloric intake per marcher.[25]

Although the Gila River plan was a risky failure, there were apparently no professional repercussions. The trip to California not only proved a professional learning experience, but it also left a major impression on Stoneman's private life. While stationed at a little outpost known as El Monte, in the hills surrounding Los Angeles, he found his natural respite. The time spent in California allowed Stoneman to foster local connections that would come to fruition following the American Civil War, where his postbellum career climaxed with his tenure as the helmsman of the future state. The subsequent decade spread Stoneman's military career wide, as the young lieutenant negotiated the traditional gauntlet of isolated stations throughout the American West that had come to be common stops along the career path of an antebellum officer. However, by the onset of the American Civil War, the freshly anointed Captain Stoneman found himself as the occupant of a critical office in the Second United States Cavalry, a regiment whose muster roll included such notables as Albert Sydney Johnston, Robert E. Lee, John Bell Hood, Earl Van Dorn and Kirby Smith.[26]

As the senior member of Company E, Stoneman built a reputation among his regimental contemporaries as an aggressive hands-on cavalry commander who delighted in personally overseeing detailed scouting expeditions via ornate marching plans, demonstrating that the young officer possessed the ability to meld a grand academic understanding of cavalry tactics with a pathfinder's mentality. His new Texas command, although inundated with the mundane tasks that plagued frontier duty, did provide the future general with his first foray into combat. The stoic New Yorker's trial by fire took the form of a series of quasi-sanctioned cross-border incursions against Mexican banditos in 1859, a daring use of initiative that received much attention from desk-bound superiors in Washington and

Austin. Confronting a continuous series of cross-border raids into frontier Texas, Stoneman liberally enforced his mandate to scout the border by leading his company on an impromptu invasion of Mexico, piercing as deep as twenty miles into the wilds of Coahuila without orders or retribution from his superiors. Although only one in a long line of spectacular exploits experienced during his tenure in Texas, Stoneman's military career became stagnant in the extremes of the old Southwest. However, on February 1, 1861, this putrid stagnation instantly evaporated.[27]

As it did for many men, North and South, the war transformed George Stoneman's life. The greatest conflict in American history spared him from the multi-decade purgatory of monotonous bean counting, pointless drills and unrewarding retirement as one of a multitude of faceless colonels populating the pension rolls. However, isolated in the farthest southwestern extremes of what was rapidly becoming the Confederate States of America, Stoneman's call for duty to the old flag became an epic journey.

The trouble began when Robert E. Lee was relieved as commander of the Department of Texas by an ancient secessionist by the name of David Emanuel Twiggs. The newly appointed Twiggs had every intention of surrendering the commands underneath him, and all of the accompanying stores of supplies, to the independent State of Texas. Naturally, once this plan was known, many of the Northern-born officers and soldiers were anxious to secure safe passage back to the United States. Stoneman, who was stationed along the Rio Grande and surrounded by rampant secessionists, took it upon himself to try to secure as much government property and loyal personnel

A portrait of George Stoneman taken shortly after his promotion to brigadier general of volunteers during the summer of 1861. *Courtesy of the Library of Congress.*

as possible. However, these efforts did not amount to much, since Lee, as an officer critical to the success of Stoneman's grand counter-secessionist plot, adopted a policy of neutrality during the Texas secession crisis.[28]

On the morning of February 19, David Twiggs surrendered the entirety of his command and the accompanying equipment in a prearranged conspiracy. The end result of days of treasonous negotiations with the Texans was that all troops and officers loyal to the United States were to assemble in San Antonio and then march out collectively, under a flag of truce, to naval transports awaiting them at various points along the Gulf of Mexico. However, this prearranged passive capitulation was not to be. Once the majority of loyal stragglers had arrived in San Antonio, the Texans swiftly reneged on the arrangement and forced the loyal personnel to sign parole papers, effectively taking them out of the war for two years.[29]

Although a respected officer before the secession crisis, David Emanuel Twiggs became widely reviled by regular army contemporaries for the treasonous surrender of the nineteen military installations that were under his command. *Courtesy of the Library of Congress.*

Leave Nothing for the Rebellion to Stand Upon

The irregular bands that formed the nucleus of the Confederate army in Texas were a constant threat to Stoneman's column and others attempting to escape the pitfalls of Federal service in states that had declared independence. *Courtesy of the Library of Congress.*

Stoneman, ignoring the orders to advance toward the waiting snare in San Antonio, looked for an alternate route of exodus. Already positioned along the border with Mexico, Stoneman undertook a line of march along the Rio Grande, intermittently loading his men and equipment aboard steamers and heading east down the river to the island of Brazos Santiago. Once in the vicinity of salt water, the anxious detachment made its way to the Gulf of Mexico port of Indianola, ultimately boarding the steamer *Coatzacoalcos* en route to New York via Key West and Havana, Cuba. The orderly execution of the impromptu march set a very encouraging precedent; for the first time, Stoneman's predisposition for lavish schemes in the face of great peril yielded advantageous fruit.[30]

Stoneman's improvised daring reaped huge rewards for the young officer and set him on an accelerated path up the ranks. The national emergency touched off by the secession crisis stripped the officer corps of many of its most experienced veterans and promising young neophytes, most of whom resigned after their sympathies toward secession took precedence over their sworn duty to uphold the Union. With a drought of qualified officers for the mounting number of vacancies and the attention garnered from his

The port of Indianola along the Brazos River as it appeared during the conflict. *Courtesy of the Library of Congress.*

superiors by his brazen escape from Texas, Stoneman was quickly presented with a series of advancements and lateral promotions, the first of which was a promotion to major in an impromptu battalion on May 9, 1861—arguably still a detachment of the now-defunct Second United States Cavalry. His only assignments in this capacity were to aid scouting operations along the north bank of the Potomac River and to protect the left flank of the main Federal body under Samuel Peter Heintzelman, who had been ordered to capture Arlington and Alexandria in order to end any potential Confederate claims to the capital city.[31]

The second significant juncture of Stoneman's wartime career came when West Point classmate George B. McClellan, intent on surrounding himself with as many familiar faces as possible, requested the major's transfer to his staff. This new appointment only laterally promoted him to acting assistant inspector general of the Department of Ohio, a position well suited to his calculative mind. Following the Confederate routs at Philippi and Rich Mountain, compounded by the disastrous summertime blunder by the Federal army at Manassas, McClellan was promoted to the head of the Army of the Potomac. Shortly after arriving in Washington, the freshman commander was informed by Lincoln that the foremost task of this new office was the refinement of a massive volunteer army to lead into Virginia.[32]

Leave Nothing for the Rebellion to Stand Upon

McClellan's faith in the Department of Ohio staff and his familiarity with its membership led directly to Stoneman's third promotion and the first big break in his military career. In search of a trusted individual who had experience leading men under fire and possessed the ability to coordinate widespread detachments of troopers, McClellan looked no further than his former classmate. The new darling of the faltering nation promoted Stoneman to brigadier general of volunteers and appointed him chief of cavalry for the Army of the Potomac in August 1862. This appointment proved very discouraging for the new general due to an unfortunate interpretation of the role of cavalry on the part of McClellan. The commander of the Army of the Potomac, concerned with the formation of a modern volunteer army, failed to fully understand the true breadth of the nature of cavalry, thus relegating it to an auxiliary branch of the infantry corps, reserved solely for the use of scouting, probing and courier duties.[33]

Stoneman's career under McClellan was bittersweet. As the commander of the Union cavalry in the Eastern Theater, he had authority in name alone, with actual command of his troopers falling into the hands of the infantry corps to which they were attached. Subject to this fragmentation of his command, Stoneman found himself a rather passive participant in the Peninsula Campaign, where he was relegated to scouting expeditions, advance guard skirmishing and general whipping boy for the superior Confederate cavalry under J.E.B. Stuart. Furthermore, his active participation in the grand race up the York-James Peninsula was circumvented by a catastrophic ailment that had developed through years of mounted service: the piles. This haunting affliction, which had cut many good cavalrymen down in the prime of their careers, surfaced for the first time and kept Stoneman from the warmest positions in the field.[34]

With its figurehead commander struck lame by an agonizingly embarrassing infirmity, the cavalry was notoriously unreliable during the campaign. This, of course, was no fault of Stoneman's, or any one mounted commander, but instead due to the restricting method of farming out the mounted regiments in lieu of a centralized command. The Confederates were strategically employing the opposite to their advantage. To compound the matter further, what action was experienced by the cavalry was reserved for less-experienced commanders, who primarily found themselves assigned to various details protecting the cold right flank of the army and rear-echelon duties. Following the retreat of the Army of the Potomac from the peninsula, the suffering general was

Stoneman and his staff near the vicinity of Fair Oaks, Virginia, during the Peninsula Campaign. *Courtesy of the Library of Congress.*

placed on sick leave and administrative detail. Much to his lasting regret, his hemorrhoids kept him from successfully mounting a horse during the Confederate invasion of Maryland.[35]

It would be almost a year before Stoneman returned to active duty, but the next campaign would provide him with the unified command that all Union cavalry commanders desperately desired and catapult him into the national spotlight as a scapegoat for one of the worst military disasters of the war. Stoneman's former California housemate, a voracious conspirator and dutiful administrator, Joseph Hooker, accepted the enormity of his new command with a confident air of optimism that distinguished him from his predecessors. Compiling intelligence from contraband slaves and entrenched spy networks, while utterly ignoring the faulty evidence of McClellan's golden boy of peculiarities, Allan Pinkerton, Hooker sought to devise a well-conceived battle plan that would avoid the hellish ordeal of full-on assault that had plagued the Union army prior to his tenure at the helm.[36]

Hooker instead devised a multifaceted campaign that would call on Stoneman to return to his previous capacity as a hands-on field commander, this time orchestrating a massive division-strong raid that would push well into the heartland of Virginia, severing Lee's supply lines, creating total pandemonium and perhaps, if the opportunity presented itself, piercing the deepest of Confederate defenses and threatening the Rebel capital itself. If everything went according to plan, and a certain element of luck presented itself, the raid would return with a few extra riders in bondage—perhaps even the renegade president of the Confederacy. However, in accordance with the constant bane of Stoneman's career, the best-laid plans often unravel the fastest.[37]

Hooker's plan was epic in scale. It called for the main body, consisting of over three corps of infantry, to advance up the Rappahannock River and flank the Confederates, who would be cleverly deceived into believing that

Stoneman and his staff take the opportunity to pose for a portrait at their headquarters in Falmouth, Virginia, prior to the disastrous Chancellorsville campaign. *Courtesy of the Library of Congress.*

the general was foolish enough to attempt another frontal assault against Fredericksburg, with the remaining four reserve corps of his army remaining at Lee's front. Hooker's anvil at Fredericksburg was in place, and the gigantic hammer of the flanking maneuver would strike an unsuspecting Confederate army. Paramount to this scheme was a major independent operation by the new cavalry corps. A lightning raid under the guidance of Stoneman would sever the Confederate lines of communication with Richmond and place a division between Lee and the Confederate capital, should he decide to retreat without a fight. At the very worst, the cavalry corps would have the honor of undertaking a desperate stand against the Confederate army, allowing Hooker enough time to close the gap and launch a destructive rear assault against the fleeing enemy.[38]

The plan of action had all the hallmarks of Hooker's masterful grasp of administration and his reckless abandon. The order of battle called for Stoneman to take command of an independent cavalry division—consisting of the majority of five brigades of volunteer cavalry regiments and their batteries, which had been recently transferred from their tenure in limbo as infantry support—and personally direct their operations in the field. Furthermore, his command was augmented with a brigade of Untied States Regular Army cavalry under the hardboiled leadership of John Buford. The end result was to be the largest cavalry operation of the war, with over ten thousand mounted men, twenty-two field pieces and 275 wagons hellbent on destruction.[39]

The proposed lightning raid centered on a line of march primarily directed against the vulnerable Orange and Alexandria Railroad intersection located at the town of Gordonsville. Critical to this strategy was a new tactic developed by Stoneman, which he dubbed "bursting shell." This experiment in widespread pandemonium required the cavalry to operate out of a centralized station of command, splinter into smaller factions and head in as many directions as possible, thus achieving a plethora of secondary objectives after the primary had been accomplished. Like many of the general's actions, this grand design quickly melded into a ruinous fiasco.[40]

Torrential rains delayed the inauguration of the raid for several days and essentially castrated it, robbing the expedition of any effective potency. Finally, after suitable river crossings were secure, the raid slowly progressed as Stoneman lost his nerve. Ultimately, the only actions of consequence were the burning of a few trestles and Buford's aggressively courageous actions, which severed telegraph lines heading out of Richmond and kept the Confederate army anxiously on its toes.[41]

Right: An iconic image of Stoneman's leadership during the Chancellorsville campaign disaster, as seen through the filtered lens of *Harper's Weekly*. *Courtesy of the Library of Congress.*

Below: The advances made by General John Buford's regular army troopers along the Rappahannock River were the highlight of Stoneman's lukewarm efforts to disrupt the Confederate rear. *Courtesy of the Library of Congress.*

This freelance mediocrity took place within the backdrop of the great Union disaster that was the Chancellorsville campaign. Following the devastating defeat handed Hooker by an imaginatively risky Confederate battle plan, the powers that be looked for a scapegoat. The Army of the Potomac's patsy manifested itself in the form of a sacrificial lamb cleverly disguised as the general who had conducted the inconsequential lightning raid at a pace that would have given even a snail ample time to sightsee. Starting with direct wires to the War Department from the sore-backed patriarch of the Army of the Potomac, and eventually capturing the attention of the Northern papers, the end result of this smear campaign was the ruination of Stoneman's reputation in the Eastern Theater.[42]

The situation confronting Stoneman, following the devastating Union reversals of the summer of 1863, was not promising; almost certainly, the odds against his dismissal would not have been humored by even the most audacious of sporting men. Surprisingly, even as a universally prodded scapegoat, the general evaded court-marshal due to lack of experienced

A portrait of George Stoneman taken about the time he was transferred to the Western Theater and promoted to major general of volunteers. *Courtesy of the Library of Congress.*

administrative officers. However, his passive role in the disaster brought the general face to face with the dreaded death knell of an active officer's career: an unceremonious kick upstairs. The middle-aged Stoneman was rewarded for his painfully pensive display of nerves during the great raid by being declared the ceremonial chief of the United States Cavalry Bureau on July 24. Taking to heart that the general was disabled due to his hemorrhoids, the inflammation was cited as the reason for his relegation to desk duty by the War Department. Stoneman was cast into an assignment he simultaneously excelled at and dreadfully loathed.[43]

As in the case of his many professional rebounds, Stoneman was yet again saved from administrative purgatory by an old compatriot. At the request of John McAllister Schofield, the berated officer was transferred to the Western Theater and made the commander of the cavalry division of the Army of Ohio, where he was elevated to major general of volunteers in January 1864. By mid-spring, an increasingly confident Stoneman was ordered to accompany William Tecumseh Sherman on his final push against

While Stoneman's rocky career owed much of its survival to prewar acquaintances, none was more active in protecting the general from detractors than John Schofield. *Courtesy of the Library of Congress.*

the Southern railroad epicenter of Atlanta. The march to northeast Georgia was not without its mishaps. En route to Sherman's command, Stoneman was forced to take extraordinary measures to prevent his unruly mountain regiments, primarily loyalists from Kentucky, from deserting as they passed through familiar territory bound for the impending slaughter in Georgia. Like his Mexican War experience with the rowdy Missourians, his relatively successful management of the flighty partisans from the borderlands provided him with the tools to hold together similar rural commands and keep them somewhat restrained in his future Carolina raid.[44]

Once in Georgia, Stoneman's haphazard misfortune disintegrated into catastrophe, as his reputation was dealt a black mark from which it never fully recovered. In July 1864, as Sherman was making his final preparations for battling the Confederate army in the vicinity of Atlanta, Stoneman presented Sherman and the War Department with one of the more ambitious plans of the conflict. Still convinced of the merits of large-scale independent cavalry actions undertaken behind enemy lines, Stoneman asked Sherman for the opportunity to raid west and southeast of Atlanta. The primary objective of this latest incarnation of a "bursting shell" was complete amputation of vital Confederate railway tethers linking Savannah and Augusta with the prize of Atlanta. With any luck, confusion created by a horde of marauding raiders

Andersonville Prison in 1864, commonly known on both sides as a deepening abyss of despair. *Courtesy of the Library of Congress.*

within the interior lines would provide Stoneman the opportunity to salvage his reputation by either forcing the complete desertion of Atlanta or assuming the mantle of liberator of the notorious Confederate hellhole halfheartedly disguised as a prison at Andersonville. However, the beleaguered general was once again subject to the disapproval of fate.[45]

The raid quickly unraveled into the perfect embodiment of total calamity. For the second time in his rocky wartime career, Stoneman was at the mercy of his two most adamant foes: inclement weather and the piles. Once again, the general became overly cautious, arguably due to his crippling condition, and his timidity cost him the crucial elements of surprise and expedience. However, the fates were not as kind to Stoneman this time around. Unlike his experiences in Virginia, which were checked primarily by the elements and a few scattered Confederate cavalry regiments, Stoneman's woes were exacerbated by an unrelenting Georgian with New England ties by the name of Joseph Wheeler.[46]

Under constant harassment from the unrelenting Confederate equestrian master and unprecedented inclement weather, Stoneman became dangerously separated from Sherman's army. Desperate for a way out of this current conundrum, Stoneman was cornered near Macon, where he had just missed a train full of the coveted Federal prisoners by a meager twelve hours. Presented with the only viable option of a lightning-quick lunge toward Union lines, Stoneman found himself cornered, not by his arch nemesis Joseph Wheeler, but instead by three brigades of Confederate infantry under Alfred Iverson. After the quick action undertaken on that particular July 27, the general made the most heartbreaking decision of his entire professional career, surging the very ranks of the Union prisoners he so desperately wanted to liberate in lieu of subjecting his command to a Thermopylae-style stand against superior numbers. While his wilder, Kentucky-born elements sought to break out with mixed results, the end result of the midsummer ignominy was that Stoneman achieved a notorious distinction that he never lived down, becoming the highest-ranking prisoner of war the Union ever relinquished to the Confederacy.[47]

Following three months as a guest of the Confederacy at both Rough and Ready, Georgia, and Charleston, South Carolina, Stoneman was exchanged for Confederate general Daniel Chevilette Govan. However, his release from imprisonment was not one of necessity or Southern benevolence; rather, it had to do with the political stance that he and two other officers took toward the Lincoln administration's policy of nonintercourse with the Confederate government over the issue of black soldiers as prisoners of war. In a letter

The superior accommodations of the racetrack clubhouse in Charleston, South Carolina, were utilized by the Confederates to house high-value prisoners like Stoneman. *Courtesy of the Library of Congress.*

dated August 14, 1864, Stoneman made a heartfelt protest, outlined in a thesis, which argued that the mobility of slavery presented black combatants with an avenue of eventual escape that put them at an advantage over their fellow white combatants relegated to the inhumane captivity of the Southern prison camps. Surely facing the soldier's silent death of permanent administrative assignment or, worse, dismissal from duty, Stoneman's reputaion was once again rescued by his old allies. The end result of War Department wrangling was his transfer to the inactively mundane theater of East Tennessee under the suspiciously watchful eyes of General Schofield.[48]

However, an impatient War Department was not pacified. With Stoneman's reputation in tatters and an ill-fated letter ordering his permanent dismissal en route from the secretary of war (later pigeonholed by his protector John Schofield), this brevetted blind squirrel finally found a nut in another professional gamble that netted great laurels: the 1865 winter raid on Saltville, Virginia. This raid against the last major salt deposit of the Confederacy, crucial for preserving the ever-dwindling stores of Rebel rations, finally proved that the concept of fast-moving and isolated raiding could be successful. After the swift destruction of the facilities and an even quicker dispatching of its defenders, the raiders returned safely without delay. The success of the raid was a bittersweet redemption for both the Union army in East Tennessee and its hierarchy.[49]

The Saltville complex had become notorious within the East Tennessee commands. That pervious October, General Stephen Burbidge led elements of the Twelfth Ohio, Eleventh Michigan, First Kentucky and Fifth United States Colored troops into Virginia with the intention of destroying the saltworks. On October 2, the column was repulsed in front of Saltville by General John C. Breckenridge. In a series of events that culminated in what Civil War sage Bell Wiley described as the only legitimate massacre of the war, large numbers of soldiers from the Fifth U.S. Colored Troops were murdered on the battlefield as they begged for quarter or were shot down in cold blood at the field hospital after the conflict.[50]

Overriding this atrocity were the actions of a local partisan by the name of Champ Ferguson, who by all accounts was a lower-class mountaineer who had sworn a blood feud against Elza Smith, a Southern-born lieutenant in the First Kentucky, for abusing his wife and daughter. On the battlefield, Ferguson was observed killing upwards of fifty-three wounded or unarmed black men. Finally, making his way to the field hospital, he found the object of his desire, Smith. Tradition holds that he had to pull the trigger three times to discharge the bullet that killed his adversary—and afterward dispatched several other wounded white and black men. The notoriety of Ferguson's breakdown was so well documented that a year later he became one of only two men executed for war crimes in the course of the entire conflict; the other, of course, was the notorious commandant of Andersonville Prison, Henry Wirz.[51]

Stoneman's vengeful descent upon the same fortifications on December 17 and 18 brought further closure to the issue of the saltworks, not only militarily, as the production facility was rendered totally impotent, but also by providing the psychological satisfaction of extracting revenge on the same fortification that had provided the backdrop for such needless slaughter. The end result of his success were glowing accolades and the casual dismissal of the orders for his termination. With his tenure in the army secure, Stoneman began to prepare for the campaign that would cement his reputation as a competent cavalry commander in the annals of the war: the exhaustive spring raid into the inactive upland regions of Confederate Carolina.

"The Union Men of East Tennessee Are Longing and Praying for the Hour When They Can Break Their Fetters"

C hrist, I'm cold." The rain beaded down on the slumped silhouette of what could best be described as a quivering scarecrow. The vacant stare, affixed intently upon an imaginary object in the distance, bore all the hallmarks of a lunatic in the midst of a surrealistic nightmare. "Please, Lord, let this rain hold out, don't let it change over." In a sigh of apathetic desperation, the remorseful prayer of the disenchanted schizophrenic was murmured: "You have made me bear too much these last few years, don't give me another night of slush; make it hold out, please don't change over."

The weathered man clung tightly to a rubber blanket with his wind-burned left hand. The glistening, chilled rain slick had been thrown over his shoulders just a few moments earlier, as the freezing rain began to plummet from an angry heaven. The back of his neck, with its tiny hairs distended to their farthest reaches, was exposed to the increasing trickle of water, which steadily worsened into a stream. The end result of the his hypothermic misery was the wrenching of his body into the stoop-shouldered stature of a frozen man, brought about by some inherent animalistic instinct that sacrificed his saturated back for a dry brow. Consequently, this contortion facilitated a cascade of water from the brim of his forward-tilted hat that anointed the unfortunate mane of his mount.

In such miserable weather, his vulcanized covering amounted to little more than an aesthetic ruse. Within the course of a quarter hour, his indigo-tinted great coat was profoundly darkened from the waist up due to its saturation. As the temperature collapsed into the nether reaches of the thermometer, the inevitable transformation of precipitation began. Quickly, the deluge of frigid liquid morphed into a blended quandary of ice and wet snow. With no foreseeable alternative to his misery, the old soldier was now resigned to his fate: "Fifteen more minutes and this whole road will be slush."

"Sergeant Anderson, move your section along." The unseen specter, possibly a lieutenant, almost inaudibly taunted the trooper as he passed by at a swift gallop. "Forward trot, march," automatically murmured the anguished soul. After three years, these words seemed to take on a life of their own—a soulless kneejerk reaction of the senses. As his right wrist lowered, the jolt of his mount, exhibiting the same defeated apathy toward its fate, jostled the rider's senses free of their misery. Surging with adrenaline, the resonation in his loins of a new campaign underway began to corkscrew up his spine. Lamenting his waterlogged predicament, his mind focused on the peculiarities of the task at hand. "I have been underway before, but this time is different."

Indeed it was. The sensation of exceptionality was the result of the mind's continuous concentration on a rather queer collection of implements issued to him just a few hours earlier at Morristown. The four auxiliary horseshoes were a clear sign that it was expected that the mounts would be driven to the point of replacement at one point along the course of the raid. Furthermore, the hollow feeling left within the trooper as a result of being ordered to strip his mount of everything but the most crucial of implements to make room for an inundation of ammunition, rations and fodder was a foreboding sign of the events to come. As the sergeant's mind began to place all the pieces of the puzzle into their proper positions, he realized that the conspicuous absence of mules, wagons and artillery pieces in the column was a sure sign that this was to be a long, hard ride.

Looking up from his sleet-blistered eyes, it became obvious that the long-lost deities were not listening to his desperate pleas for obedience. The sergeant could see the faint glows of lanterns in the distance, indicative that the entire mounted column stretched to the edges of the highland horizon. The intermittent flashes of white, mixed in with the hazy fog of freezing rain, served as a veil, which covered the flickering beams of light that laboriously snaked up Bull's Gap along the Babb's Mill Road and finally disappeared around the bend into a blank and seeming nothingness. This eerie scene, only exacerbated by the driving, freezing rain, sleet and wet snow, presented an illusion reminiscent of Dante's trek through the circles of hell.[52]

Everett W. Anderson, one of many introspective sufferers lost in the column of thousands, was a man who was accustomed to combat. Having been in the saddle with the Fifteenth Pennsylvania Cavalry since 1862, he had experienced very warm action in both major theaters of the war. Thirty years removed from his present frigid situation, Anderson was awarded the Congressional Medal of Honor rather unexpectedly for a haphazard stroke of luck that was bestowed on him by the same deities that were presently focusing their amusement on his anguish. On a wet January afternoon the previous year at Crosby Creek, Tennessee, he had opportunistically come face to face with Confederate general Robert B. Vance during a confusingly swift charge against the general's Tennessee cavalry. In the heat of the moment, the sergeant had pressed his ranked adversary to surrender—in the sergeant's mind, one gilded prisoner in a herd of dozens.[53]

Despite the confusion, only one fact remained constant: it was March 23 outside of Morristown, Tennessee, and the sergeant's crack troops were underway to yet another undisclosed location. By his assumptions, the objective was most likely Asheville, North Carolina, by some roundabout northwestern route. However, the veteran could not have hedged his wager further from the truth, as the secretive mission would consume nearly three months of the sergeant's life. This hellish endeavor would last from March until June and spread Anderson's weary bones over five hundred miles of roads that dissected the landscape of four rebellious states. By the time the first day of summer witnessed his muster out of the Union army at Nashville, the late-hour raid had become a suitable capstone to his military career. Finally, collecting one last deep breath of the sweet air of a mountain summer afternoon, the sergeant could take solace in the fact that he had been a member of the marauding faction that had castrated the dying rebellion, had greatly assisted in rounding up the last remnants of the renegade Confederate chain of command and had unleashed the unholy specter of open war against noncombative civilians in a docile theater, ultimately bringing the Rebels to the realization that they were, in fact, defeated, regardless of not having been exposed to the horrors of war.[54]

The miserable contingent of men who slowly trotted east from Morristown, hellbent for Boone, North Carolina, were the core elements of a "bursting shell"-style raid into the eastern Appalachian rim of the Confederacy. In the greater scheme of the aging conflict, Stoneman's latest tenure in the saddle was only one of the three proposed grand western raids into the crippled Confederacy during the spring of 1865. The easternmost prong of the triple assault on the Confederacy led by Stoneman was a proposed raid from East

In conjunction with the efforts of Stoneman, troopers under James Harrison Wilson were to strike out and render the last havens of the dying Confederacy useless to the shrinking Rebel army. *Courtesy of the Library of Congress.*

Like his two counterparts, Edward Canby was successful in inflicting late-hour damage on his ailing adversary. *Courtesy of the Library of Congress.*

Tennessee into the mountains of North Carolina, ultimately bringing the war to the unaffected upstate boroughs of South Carolina. Coupled with two other ventures into the Deep South, James H. Wilson's push into central Alabama by way of Tuscaloosa and Selma and Edward R.S. Canby's push against the coastal stronghold of Mobile, these detailed raids were designed to weed out the last of the Confederate holdouts and leave the last few unaffected coves of the South with a true sense of desolation.[55]

However, well-laid plans are subject to the forces of chance and nature. Upon being informed of the potential raid on January 31, via a telegraph from Ulysses S. Grant, Stoneman enthusiastically went to work orchestrating his latest grandiose design. Wiring George H. Thomas on the matter, Stoneman requested two thousand fresh mounts, six hundred Spencer repeating rifles and the consolidation of a number of the local "Home Yankee" regiments, which would then be reorganized to serve as the heart of Stoneman's new command. Naturally, the moniker "Home Yankee" was unfairly saddled to those mountaineers from Kentucky, North Carolina and Tennessee who chose to remain loyal to the old flag—a designation that was the source of tremendous strife during the war and great myth afterward. With an air of enthusiasm toward the swift and successful departure of the new adventure

Virginia native and Western Theater hero George H. Thomas was instrumental in keeping the turbulent Stoneman actively in the saddle, even as his superiors dismissed the New Yorker as a nonentity. *Courtesy of the Library of Congress.*

spreading to other high-ranking officers in Thomas's department, Stoneman was reassured that he would have his consolidation of mountaineers and the requested fresh equipment in ten to fifteen days. However, the expedient execution of the raid that encouraged this air of optimism was not to be.[56]

A full six weeks after being notified of the task at hand and the completion of the various requisitions for pertinent accoutrements, Stoneman found himself still wasting away in Knoxville without any of the aforementioned materials that he had solicited from the War Department. Dividing the interim weeks between the "Home Yankee" elements of his command that had assembled at Louisville, Kentucky, and his veteran soldiers stationed at Knoxville, Tennessee, Stoneman was haunted by the ragged shape of his troopers. His men were without proper arms, mounts and materials, and even more importantly, discipline was eroding by the second. All of this resulted in an unforeseen delay that garnered the attention of the War Department, which instantly made demands for explanations about why his command was collecting dust and not reducing the Confederate infrastructure to cinders. The delay was devastating to his crumbling reputation and the tedious commission that held it together. While excuses abounded, one constant remained clear: as the nature of the war was changed, his command collected dust. Once again, the ill-fated New Yorker found himself victim to the new foe of circumstantial lethargy.[57]

As the crucial moments ticked by, Stoneman's mission and its original definition profoundly evolved as the war experienced a substantial metamorphosis during the first few months of 1865. The original intention of the raid, as devised by General Grant, called for Stoneman to leave Knoxville and to penetrate South Carolina as deep as Columbia in auxiliary support of Sherman's Carolina invasion. Consequently, men and materials would be drawn away from the path of resistance to Sherman. In the process, Stoneman was to destroy as many railroad and military resources as his command could happen upon in the upstate of South Carolina. As Grant correctly surmised, the upstate would be relatively undefended, which only served to exacerbate his frustration with Stoneman's inaction due to reduced strength and lack of proper equipment. At one point, Grant explicitly expressed doubt that the Confederates possessed a force in the entirety of the region that could not be vested successfully with little more than fifteen hundred men.[58]

In the air of optimism that accompanied the planning stages of the raid, Grant suggested that while the main Confederate body was busy with Sherman, the auxiliary raiders might even be fortunate enough to slip into west-central North Carolina and liberate the last major Confederate prison at Salisbury. However this optimism, for the moment at least, proved short-lived and unwarranted. By the time the charred remnants of Columbia were in Union hands, Stoneman's raid into the Carolinas was still a pipe dream. Disgusted with the inaction, Grant openly lamented that the only good that could come from the lethargic Stoneman's venture into South Carolina was to destroy frivolous stock.[59]

At the time the raid was implemented, the military situation had changed dramatically. By March 19, Grant was directly ordering Stoneman to throw whatever forces he had in his possession against Western North Carolina and southwest Virginia immediately, thus completely discarding the thoroughly planned operation. This came as no surprise, particularly since the original intention of the raid was now obsolete, due to Sherman's progression through the Carolinas. However, Grant's angst was only a few hours unwarranted, as the raid was already halfheartedly inaugurated under the direction of Stoneman's second in command, who was leading the nine-regiment assembly out of Knoxville at the bequest of Stoneman, and was bound for Morristown for a final refitting before undertaking the monumental task. While the column was underway during his absence, Stoneman arrived at the head of the column on March 20.[60]

The plan of action, now dictated to Stoneman by Grant via George H. Thomas, was to proceed up the New River Valley out of East Tennessee, rendering the East Tennessee and Virginia Railroad on the western side of Christiansburg, Virginia, useless to the Army of Northern Virginia. Such an action would essentially rob Robert E. Lee of any possible avenue of resupply west of Petersburg due to the increasing likelihood that the siege would be ending there. More importantly, a successful operation would prevent the railway line from facilitating his escape should he desire to use Western North Carolina as the rallying point for his shattered army. In a sense, the raid, coordinated with the efforts of other Union commands, would create the bag that Marse Robert would be driven into by a pursuing Grant. If all went according to plan, the troublesome and unfortunate Stoneman could finally demonstrate his worth to the high command.[61]

The cavalry division that the United States Army unleashed on the communities east of the crest of the Blue Ridge was mammoth. The six thousand men whose destinies were intertwined with that of the haphazard New Yorker consisted of nine regiments divided into three brigades of relatively equal size. The operational commander of the division whose men composed the vast majority of the charge presented to George

Hailing from East Tennessee, Alvan Gillem was intimately familiar with the nature of the war as it was understood in the Appalachian Mountains. While often dismissed as an outright pirate by many in Confederate Appalachia, he was instrumental in the Unionist efforts of the region. *Courtesy of the Library of Congress.*

Stoneman was a Tennessee loyalist from Gainesboro by the name of Alvan Cullem Gillem.[62]

Gillem, who was politically ambitious and opportunistic during the conflict, had remained loyal to the old flag. His decision to retain his allegiance to the United States was largely influenced by his personal loyalties toward his old friend George H. Thomas, who solicited his help in organizing loyalists in the region after his native state seceded from the Union. As a native of East Tennessee, Alvan Gillem was affected by the cultural divisions that had been present in the state since its founding. Largely a nonparticipant in the cotton culture that dominated the remainder of the state, the mountainous eastern portion of Tennessee remained impoverished, culturally independent and bitterly resentful toward its antebellum counterparts outside of Appalachia. Fully understanding these cultural divisions, Gillem threw in his hat with the government best suited for his people and his career.[63]

Reorganizing northeast of Knoxville along the railway trestle on the outskirts of Strawberry Plains, the division finalized its command structure.

The First Brigade of the division, constituting the majority of the non-native soldiers in the whole expedition, consisted of the Twelfth Ohio, Tenth Michigan and Fifteenth Pennsylvania. The trio fell under the watchful eye of William J. Palmer, a conditionally pacifist Quaker emancipationist who hailed from Leipsic, Delaware. In the years preceding the war, he had built a name for himself in the field of railroad promotion; however, this temporary career as a promoter was cut short by the onset of the war and an opportunity to follow his true calling: freeing the bonded from their tumultuous burdens.

The Second Brigade was an odd collection of a handful of mountaineer regiments from the Bluegrass State who found themselves paired with one tempered regiment hailing from north of the Mason-Dixon line. The members of the Eleventh and Twelfth Kentucky Cavalry regiments were noted for being reckless and disorderly on the campaign. Therefore, Stoneman saw fit to pair the two with the veteran Eleventh Michigan, in hopes that the regiment could lead the brigade by example. The man picked to lead the ensemble, Simeon B. Brown, was a tall and picturesque personage of military manner with a chin beard. Prior to the outbreak of hostilities, he busied himself with the operation of his hotel at Saint Clair, Michigan, where he pursued an amateur interest in local politics. Naturally, Brown made no reservations in hiding the fact that, like so many of his counterparts, he intended the war to serve as a springboard to wider political success.[64]

Stoneman's Third Brigade, the representative embodiment of much of the lowland South's angst, troubled the inhabitants of Confederate Appalachia the most by far. Comprising local "Home Yankees" from both sides of the Blue Ridge, this cadre of regiments had the most to gain from the potential social realignment that a Union victory in the war would bestow upon the South. As residents of a marginalized region of the cotton kingdom, these soldiers were driven by a multitude of incentives. While the conflict provided these men with an opportunity to exact a little retribution against the social imbalance of the antebellum South, which showed favoritism toward eastern North Carolina and western Tennessee, it also presented a chance for them to advance their economic positions through pillage. Cut from the same homespun cloth as mountain loyalists Andrew Johnson and George H. Thomas, the men who rode with the Eighth, Ninth and Thirteenth Tennessee Cavalry regiments had long garnered notoriety for their use of brute tactics and ferocious thievery against mountain supporters of the Confederacy.[65]

This cavalcade of local soldiers was fortunate enough to have one of their own to serve as helmsman—John K. Miller, a native of East Tennessee. At

The behind-doors Unionist meeting was a common occurrence in the Appalachian counties of North Carolina and Tennessee. Many of these meetings' participants would eventually fill the ranks of dozens of loyalist regiments mustered throughout Appalachia. *Courtesy of the Library of Congress.*

the outbreak of hostilities, Miller occupied the position of sheriff in Carter County, Tennessee, and helped to secure arms for local resistance to the newly formed Confederate authorities in East Tennessee. During the brief civil war waged in East Tennessee, tepidly fought within the backdrop of the emerging national rebellion, Miller was instrumental in securing a series of critical railway trestles from the malevolent designs of local Confederate saboteurs. The fact that these infrastructures were left intact greatly aided George H. Thomas in his swift occupation of the region and brought Miller to the attention of loyalist state leaders. Following an appointment as quartermaster for loyalist militias in the region, his rise to prominence among state loyalists began in earnest when he personally organized local volunteers into the Thirteenth Tennessee Cavalry regiment at Strawberry Plains in the autumn of 1863.[66]

The loyalist overtones of the raid became obvious at Morristown, Tennessee, as the column rode into the town on March 23 to much fanfare and warm accolades from the local citizens. However, the pleasantries afforded the raiders at Morristown were not to be savored, as the men were swiftly marched through the town and into the rolling countryside. On the

HARPER'S WEEKLY.
JOURNAL OF CIVILIZATION.
Vol. VI.—No. 274.] NEW YORK, SATURDAY, MARCH 29, 1862. [SINGLE COPIES SIX CENTS.

Left: Having been overshadowed by the paternalist cotton culture of the lowland South for generations, many of the Unionists in the higher elevations were vehement in their commitment to fight the secession movement and the growing rebellion. *Courtesy of the Library of Congress.*

Below: A lithograph detailing the growing collection of local residents buried in Knoxville who gave their lives in the struggle to preserve the Union. *Courtesy of the Library of Congress.*

The hotly contested trestle at Strawberry Plains, Tennessee, served as the staging ground for many Unionist raids into western North Carolina. *Courtesy of the Library of Congress.*

eastern outskirts of town, the column was dismounted and refitted at the last moment to ensure that the men would have adequate provisions for the adventure. Included in the parting equipment issuance were the infamous four horseshoes, accompanying nails and one hundred cartridges that were widely remembered by the survivors of the adventure.[67]

Having learned through the trials of the previous three years, the column assembling outside of Morristown was devoid of the opulent bells and whistles of the previous Stoneman adventures. The general, who customarily hindered the expedient potential of his command with burdensome auxiliary muleskinners driving files upon files of quartermaster wagons and ambulances, deprived his new command of any semblance of strategic reserve. The entire column of six thousand men was supplemented with a lean collection of one wagonload of critical supplies, ten ambulances and four limbered guns, all of which was swiftly discarded once the column began to encounter delays wrought by poor road conditions.[68]

Attempting to add fuel to the smoldering confusion that was beginning to grip the Confederate high command, Stoneman divided his army in an attempt to mask the true intentions of his raid. At Bull's Gap, Stoneman separated his command into two wings. The main body, consisting of a pairing of the First and Second Brigades under the direct command of the old man himself, took the most direct route to the east by way of the Babb's Mill Road toward Jonesboro, Tennessee. All the while, the Third Brigade, under Colonel Miller, took a wayward path that followed the Watauga River and arrived at Jonesboro via Carter's Station.

It was along the river that a contingent of the Third Brigade drew the first blood of the raid when it engaged, charged and routed unorganized rabble consisting of about sixty men attached to the notorious East Tennessee Confederate Cavalry menace General John C. Vaughn. While the butcher bill was clean for the raiders, the men took four prisoners in the process and possibly wounded a few Rebel troopers, establishing a relatively bloodless precedent that held true for the majority of the marathon campaign. The

Having been witness to the bombardment of Fort Sumter as a civilian, John Crawford Vaughn remained in Confederate service until the very end by serving as one of President Jefferson Davis's escorts on his failed bid to elude capture. *Unknown source.*

ruse intended by splintering the division worked, and the Confederate high command was inundated with correspondence arguing that an invasion of central Western North Carolina toward Asheville was imminent. Nary a word concerning the irreplaceable railway links of southwestern Virginia was mentioned, a sure sign that they were hardly considered targets.[69]

While the departure from Morristown was executed under fair weather, the situation rapidly deteriorated as inclement weather set in. After two days of slow going along the muddy terrain, the First and Second Brigades found themselves ten miles short of Jonesboro. Frustrated by the snail's pace, Stoneman ordered his column to halt and issued all the provisions that his men could functionally carry from his lumbering supply wagon. Early on the morning of March 26, the wagon and ambulances were turned back, and the column advanced into Jonesboro unencumbered by the burden of the ration-laden albatrosses. Colonel Miller of the Third Brigade was waiting in Jonesboro with his command and the unfortunate information that the railroad trestle spanning the Watauga River was severely damaged and doomed any opportunity to resupply or retire the raid by rail. When the news of this development reached Knoxville, a large support operation to secure the interior lines of the raid was undertaken to ensure that the basic routes of retreat and resupply were unhampered—a cautious nod by the high command of the Department of Tennessee to Stoneman's notorious tendency toward disastrous retreat.[70]

As the troopers began moving toward the Blue Ridge, the personal nature of the raid took hold as elements of true civil war began to emerge. Since the vast majority of Stoneman's command were considered to be "Home Yankees," it was well understood that a watchful eye was to be cast upon the collection of troopers whose own eyes were smoldering with the fanatical embers of revenge. More telling of the anti-antebellum establishment overtones of the raid was the widespread participation of civilians throughout the various coves in aiding the troopers' safe passage. As the riders crossed over into North Carolina, by way of the isolated outpost of Banner Elk, the martial travelers of the precarious roads that snaked through the mountains were met with the queerest of sights.[71]

In the forty-eight miles the command had traversed since leaving Jonesboro on the twenty-sixth, not a single Confederate loyalist had crossed their path. Instead, as frigid weather set in once again on the twenty-eighth, the precarious state of the road became an inevitable hindrance to the progression of the column. However, without solicitation, numerous locals began to line the steep roads of the gap and build fires along the rim of the cliffs at points where the road would instantaneously transform into open air. Although a cannon caisson and a mule team were lost following the collapse of a steep bank under its massive weight, not a single man was harmed in the crossing of the crest.[72]

As one survivor remembered:

> *Many local citizens built fires along the road and at dangerous places, and also at difficult fords over the mountain streams. Looking back as we toiled up the mountain, the scene was grand and imposing as the march of the column was shown the trail of fire along the road. Occasionally an old pine tree would take fire and blaze up almost instantaneously, looking as a column of fire. It was an impromptu illumination, and the sight of it repaid us after the toilsome night march.*[73]

The advance lasted into the day-clean hours, and about four o'clock in the morning on the twenty-eighth, the column halted for a tantalizing break. However, by eight o'clock the column was once again underway and bound for Sugar Grove. The soggy troopers arrived shortly after one o'clock in

A field sketch of the precarious nighttime travel to which many troopers were subjected along the Blue Ridge. *Courtesy of the Library of Congress.*

the afternoon, where they were rewarded for their exhaustive labors with a break just slightly under an hour. Following their arousal from a very hasty slumber, the column advanced southward in the direction of the village of Banner Elk. The ride was pleasant, as the whole county was inundated by loyalists, with only one identified Confederate family residing in the area. While the willful support of the people for the column was perhaps little more than innocent opportunism, the population had suffered heavily at the hands of renegade Confederate home guardsmen over the previous few years and was no doubt ecstatic to see the stability of the Union army enter into its coves. As the riders progressed, local citizens willfully provided the column with guides and materials, a clear sign that they were finally choosing a side and casting their lots with the victorious raiders.[74]

As the column wound through the mountains, the first victims of the raid were about to have their false sense of security rocked to its core foundation. For the hamlet of Boone, North Carolina, the war had only brought the occasionally rare, sporadic and inconsequential raid by bushwhacker bands or loyalist paramilitary organizations. However, on the morning of March 8, the county seat of Watauga County was about to experience a rude awakening. By midmorning, elements of the Twelfth Kentucky Cavalry, led by Major Myles Keogy, unexpectedly crashed down on an assembly of home guardsmen on the outskirts of Boone.[75]

This assembly of local amateur soldiers was by no means an equal match. A few weeks earlier, their sister company had surrendered to loyalist elements in the Thirteenth Tennessee without a fight, and now the remaining organization within the borders of Watauga County was assembling at Boone after the alarm had been sounded that another band of opportunistic bushwhackers was marauding through the vicinity. Unfortunately for the faux soldiers, their misinformation perpetuated their demise. Convinced that the ruffians rounding the bend in piecemeal fashion were most likely renegade bands of deserters, or worse, a few loosely organized loyalist squads bent on financial acumen, the home guard opened fire on the lead echelons of the column.[76]

For many years, the origins of the engagement outside Boone had been hotly contested, as many were in disagreement over what had inaugurated the row. Local lore states that the home guardsmen assembled in the field along the road into town were by no means ready, or looking, for a fight with hardened Union veterans. As the men began to disperse, one of the amateurs accidentally let his hammer fall from the safety position onto the primer cap, thus igniting the cartridge resting inside the barrel. The accidental report was quickly answered by a volley of repeating rifle fire from the files of

A period sketch of Union cavalry advancing across a mountain pasture in skirmish formation. *Courtesy of the Library of Congress.*

advancing cavalry scouts. The retribution was swift and accurate. As the home guardsmen discharged their muskets at the advancing scout troop, they were met with an unceasing hail of lead, which led the majority to take flight for the screen of trees directly to their rear. When the minor scrape was over, local lore held that three militiamen were killed—although Stoneman reported that his troopers felled nine home guardsmen. Only a solitary slain raider was reported by either side.[77]

As the vanguard advanced across the field, a fifteen-year-old junior reserve by the name of Steel Frazier vaulted a fence and took position behind a post. Drawing a careful bead on one of the charging troopers, he coolly squeezed the trigger. His ball flew true and instantly dropped the lead rider from his mount. Either distracted by the scattering of the frightened home guard to the four corners of the field or unable to place the exact location of the unseen enemy, the troopers failed to react, and Frazier was able to ram yet another round down his barrel and place a cap on the vent. Taking quick and precise aim, he fired off another round, yet again downing a rider, and this time dispatched his victim. Knowing that his luck would not hold out, the young man took for the tree line as the surviving raiders pursued him while firing. Nimble enough to avoid the shots of the troopers that were bearing down on him, Frazier managed to reach the wood line and soon lost his pursuers in the thick cluster of firs and hardwoods.[78]

With their blood up, the raiders poured into Boone expecting to fight their first substantial engagement of the operation. Unfortunately for the town's people, the home guard had no intention of continuing its newfound bad luck against the troopers and was now nervously seeking refuge in the surrounding hillsides and forests. Spoiling for a fight, and with none to be found, the troopers turned their attention to the local inhabitants. Unbeknownst to Jacob M. Council, who was busying himself and his manservant with the plowing of one of his fields, the raiders were bearing down on them.

As the troopers crossed into Council's field, the pair froze at the plow. The soldiers quickly surrounded them, and then, for some unknown reason, his slave screamed to the edgy raiders that this man was an infernal Rebel. The accusation was quickly followed with a volley of fire that cut down the aging noncombatant. While local historians took pains to document the ills that befell Jacob M. Council on that unfortunate day, little was mentioned of the demise of the other civilian casualty. As in the case of Jacob Council, Warren Greene was unnecessarily slain as he attempted to prevent the theft of his livestock from his barn at the hands of greedy raiders. Unconcerned with the rights of personal property, one raider cut the man down with unabashed disregard for life as he reached for the halter of his prized mount.[79]

The mistreatment of noncombatants did not end on the outlying fields of the village, as the raiders made their ill intentions equally known to the townies. Survivors of that damp morning recalled how utterly surprised they were at the arrival of the troopers and at the swiftness with which the town was engulfed by the command. As the troopers rode down Main Street, they were said to have fired at everything and everyone who crossed their path with no demands for surrender or quarter falling from their mouths. Rushing to her piazza to see what the commotion was about, the wife of James Council was met by a volley of fire that shattered her windows and ate away at the wood siding. Although nearly a dozen projectiles flew toward her, the woman escaped without physical injury, suffering only the loss of her nerves as she rushed back to a secluded room in her house.[80]

But the mistreatment did not stop there. Running through the streets, Calvin Greene was headed off by a trooper, who forced him to surrender. As Greene threw his hands into the air, the demanding trooper unceremoniously shot him in the chest. While Greene was left for dead in the street, and little hope was given to his survival after the departure of the column, the man eventually recovered from his wounds to spend several more decades in the village.[81]

As the main column rode into Boone, the effectiveness of the home guard's impromptu battle became apparent as the house of Jordon D. Council was converted into a makeshift hospital, which was quickly populated with five troopers, who were treated for wounds sustained in the mêlée that occurred on the outskirts of the village. While the village began to be swarmed with the mounted men, officers paid little heed to the actions of their troopers. The men, particularly those who belonged to elements of the Twelfth Kentucky, began to loot and selectively enter the more luxurious houses in search of whatever valuables caught their fancy. In the name of liberating the people from the secessionist government, General Gillem ordered the county jail and all Confederate records burned in mass. This action, which greatly impedes historians of the region due to the fact that many of the records from the early republic were also put to the torch, were widely rebuked by General Stoneman once he arrived on the scene.[82]

The violent heralding of the raid into North Carolina was one that was never forgotten. The day had been eventful and bloody. The butcher bill for the morning witnessed nine home guardsmen killed, sixty-two captured and forty horses confiscated. All of this was achieved at the cost of two men killed and five incapacitated from either wounds sustained in the fight or injuries incurred in the line of duty. The prisoners, some of whom were too old and infirm to even be considered combatants, were rounded up and marched west in the direction of Knoxville. The end result of their forced expatriation was an unfortunate tenure at the dreaded Camp Chase, Ohio, where local tradition holds that many died along the way or in the camp itself.[83]

One man, Lemis Farthing, found emancipation from his situation by an exercise in quick thinking. As he was being marched in line along a winding mountain road with a steep drop on the shoulder, Lemis unfurled the blanket that was strapped across his torso, nonchalantly draped it over his back and then suddenly leapt down the bank. Snagging the blanket lengthwise across a mountain laurel, he created a blind through which the troopers could not see. Their only option was to saturate the blanket and its vicinity with gunfire, which missed Lemis Farthing, who had slid down the incline in a managed freefall toward safety.[84]

Before Stoneman departed from Boone, he saw fit to ensure that his lines of retreat and resupply would be well guarded in the case of military disaster. Under the guidance of a Mainer by the name of Davis Tillson, the Department of East Tennessee made doubly sure that the marauding general's lifeline was well protected. Initially ordering a "Home Yankee" of vicious notoriety by the name of George W. Kirk to Boone from his present post along Roan Creek, Tennessee, a slew of Union men moved into the mountain passes. Kirk brought with him the Second and Third North Carolina Mounted Infantry, two regiments bursting at the seams with men from the mountains, who were looking for any opportunity to extract hardships on the Confederate elements of the region. Then again, there was Kirk, who was notorious for his sadistic pursuit of treasure and opportunities to extract vengeance against the mountain secessionists. Leaving Tennessee on April 3, the regiments arrived on the sixth and began to fortify the gaps outside Boone.[85]

Making his headquarters in the home of Jordon Council, which had just a few days earlier served as a Federal hospital, Kirk personally looted the residence and locked Mrs. Council into her room for the duration of his stay. Understanding the necessity for a base of operations in the event that

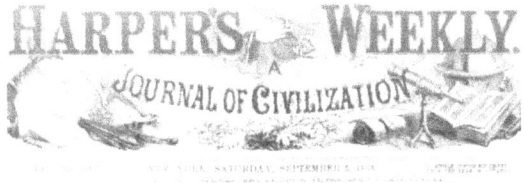

The activities of less disciplined Unionist bands, such as the one that fell under the auspices of Kirk, drew the most disdain from the Confederate inhabitants of North Carolina. *Courtesy of the Library of Congress.*

the Confederate government should attempt to push the issue brewing in the mountains, Kirk ordered his men to convert the county courthouse into a blockhouse. The swift renovation was accomplished by boarding up the windows, cutting riffle slits in the wall and throwing up defilade around the perimeter in order to discourage a besieging force from attempting to raze the impromptu fort. As other commands and artillery under General David Tillson were making their way into the North Carolina mountains, Kirk's men began to erect barricades along every major roadway, save the route from Banner Elk, which was commonly known to be exclusively Unionist. After a few days, the majority of the department was occupying every major gap in the region, including the insulting employment of the First United States Colored Heavy Artillery at Taylorsville.[86]

The raid was off to a successful start. For the first time in a major operation, George Stoneman was in the midst of a plan that was becoming fruitful through successful execution. Despite the early inclement weather and the necessity to drop his supply wagons due to poor roads, the overall timetable of the raid was still in order. However, the success of the raid would be constantly in doubt during the course of the next few weeks, as he lurched toward his first major oppositions by the determined defenders of the crucial railway lines of southwest Virginia.

3

"In Fact, I Thought Everybody around Stoneman Would Be Killed"

T he ominous, clamoring echo of hobnailed boots rushing across the pine-planked veranda toward the workroom floor heralded the imminent danger descending upon the inhabitants of Patterson's Mill, throwing them into a desperate panic. Dropping the bundle of cloth that was tucked underneath his arm, a costly exchange for the liberty of a full sprint, Clem Osborne dug his right heel into the wooden floor, pivoted and pushed off with an intensity that found him at full stride in just a matter of steps. The only fixture in the room that attracted his terror-saturated attention was the door on the eastern end of the factory floor; its pine frame and walnut knob beckoned to him as he scrambled to reach it. Osborne's attention was so fixed on his rapidly nearing idol that the cries from the men entering the room behind him were practically inaudible: "Stop you Goddamn secesh! So help me God I will shoot!"[87]

It was shortly after nine on the night of March 28, 1865, and Osborne had ventured down to Patterson's Mill along the Yadkin River to purchase several spools of thread and a bolt of cloth for assembling new articles of clothing for his family. Having worked all day around the homestead, Osborne set out for the local mill after dark to conduct his transaction. The sudden arrival of the Union troopers startled both Osborne and the proprietor of the mill into a panic. While not a supporter of secession, or a fevered loyalist, Osborne knew better than to stand idle while armed men were frantically rushing into a room. To compound the confusion of the moment even further, there was the history of the mill itself, which had been a major source of cloth for the loyalist families and militias of East Tennessee, as its owner was decidedly in the Unionist camp. With the mill having garnered such renown within Unionist circles, why the raiders decided to storm malevolently into Patterson's Mill is lost to history.

As the door drew nearer, a peculiar sensation echoed through Osborne's right ear and corkscrewed downward through his spinal column. The morbid origins of this sensation did not dawn on the man until, in the midst of his flight, he noticed a peculiarity that his eyes had never experienced previously—the doorframe was bursting into splinters before him. As his mind processed the new development, the shock delivered to his soul wrestled him free from his tunnel vision. "Oh God, they are shooting at me." Hunkering down, trying his best to shrink his body into its smallest possible silhouette, Osborne pushed harder for the battered exit.

Finally reaching the door, he burst through it by leading with his left side; no doubt, had his senses not been dulled by adrenaline, he would have certainly been hindered by his newly busted shoulder. It was there on the eastern exterior of the mill that a critical decision had to be made within the course of two footsteps: make for the woods, which lay across the road and a long, open cornfield; make for the river to his immediate left, which would leave him submerged in freezing water while simultaneously hurdling rocks; or make for another part of the factory in an effort to hide. As the loft staircase came into view to his left, the decision seemed preordained, and Osborne made for the second floor. Exerting every ounce of energy that his body could muster in order to provide enough room between himself and his pursuers, the fleeing shopper bound up the stairs two at a time. In just a few seconds, he reached the upstairs office door of the mill, and he experienced his first stroke of luck when he found the office door unlocked and slightly ajar.

Upon rushing into the center of the office, Osborne realized that his newfound sanctuary afforded him no chance of cover and that he had trapped himself like a rabbit in a log. Taking the ladder-back chair from the mill owner's desk, he instinctively wedged it tightly under the doorknob to serve as a barricade. Clearly hearing the frantic exchange between the mill owner and the troopers on the factory floor, coupled with the sound of the eastern door bursting open under the force of a trooper throwing his weight into the perforated pine planks at full speed, Osborne knew that his efforts were futile. Ransacking the office for the door key, he knew time was short, and with the pounding of boots up the loft staircase, it was only a matter of time before Osborne would once again find himself face to face with his pursuers.

Leave Nothing for the Rebellion to Stand Upon

As the raiders attempted to force open the door, which barely budged in its reinforced state, their frightened prey could hear the troopers on the opposite side, calling down to their fellow pursuers with the good news that the occupant had cornered himself and there was no need to further search the perimeter. With the realization that his flight was over, Osborne's mind began to race for any alleviation from his predicament. As the troopers began to throw their weight against the door, causing it to give way, a kneejerk reaction that had been engrained in Osborne's subconscious for over twenty years came crashing down on him, and his body instinctively conformed to the primeval orders. Drawing his feet together and folding his arms upward at right angles, then moving them in an unmentionable repetitive fashion, he greeted the entering troopers with this unexpected and unnatural gesture.[88]

Instantly, the second trooper to crest the threshold called out for his compatriots to lower their weapons, "This man is a brother, don't touch him!" The utterance of those words threw everyone in the room aback, including Osborne, whose heart was squarely lodged in the middle of his throat. In that very instant, a full half of the troopers looked at the corporal as if he were insane, while a handful nodded in agreement after catching a glimpse of their prey. After a little convincing, the non-Masonic soldiers were pacified by the queer explanations espoused by their comrades to the extent that they were willing to leave the suspect alone with the troopers who had been accepted, passed and raised in a similar fashion as the petrified man in the middle of the room.[89]

After the office door was secured to the full extent that the shattered door frame would allow, the situation relaxed itself. It was in that moment of solitude that the troopers laid their Spencer rifles against the wall and began pertinent conversation with their newfound acquaintance in hopes that a conclusion could be reached before less understanding combatants arrived at the mill. After providing the traditionally accepted answers to a memorized interrogation, which was followed by a series of ritualistic posturing, it was agreed upon by the mounted brethren that Clem Osborne was, in fact, a legitimate eastern traveler. Upon reaching this conclusion, the only course of action that could be taken under the laws of the order was safe and unhampered passage back to his home. Understanding that time was of the essence, since the entire regiment was traveling a few minutes behind the advance guard, Osborne was returned to his buggy with the contents of the sack, which he had dropped. Without so much as an apology for their poor demonstration in marksmanship and the jaw-dropping amount of lead thrown in his direction, Osborne was swiftly loosed back into the early spring night with the souvenirs of this most taxing shopping trip engrained in his memory—laying the foundation for the creation of a story that would be retold by the local populace for generations to come.[90]

This fleeting episode of personal terror, one of countless similar occurrences during the war, happened the very same day that Stoneman's command swooped down on the unsuspecting populace of Boone. The troopers who intruded on Patterson's Mill were the advance elements of Simeon B. Brown's Second Brigade, most likely Tennessee "Home Yankees." Considering the early morning row that these men had heard, witnessed or experienced outside Boone, their blood was still undoubtedly up from the column's earlier blood-soaked skirmish with the local home guard. This, of course, gave their disposition a less-than-hospitable air when they arrived at the mill. While an isolated handful of Brown's Brigade observed their Masonic obligations and allowed Clem Osborne safe passage, the mill by far fared less well.

For a time, it appeared as if the mill would stand, as those who had originally stormed the structure sought to uphold their peaceful reassurances and their private Masonic duties to the owner. Initially, the lead elements of

Falling Creek Mill outside Hickory, North Carolina, was a prime example of mill construction throughout Appalachia. *Courtesy of the Library of Congress.*

Brown's command rested along the Yadkin on the site of the mill and went as far as to organize an overzealous guard detail to prevent the pillage of the supply of cloth that rested there. However, the interest of a national war effort superseded supposed ancient fraternal orders, no matter how popular and widespread they may have been. While the soldiers stood guard and rested until shortly before noon the following morning, eventually they were presented with orders to move on along their path of march.

The brethren's successors, Colonel Miller's Third Brigade, arrived with the heartbreaking orders to burn the mill. This distasteful action was supposedly the result of a direct order from division commander General Gillem—a

The destruction of mills and infrastructure by roving cavalry bands was a tragic, yet integral, component of the Union war effort. *Courtesy of the Library of Congress.*

A field sketch of the remnants of a mill following its incineration. *Courtesy of the Library of Congress.*

directive that did not sit well with the "Home Yankee" soldiers, who were familiar with the mill's history of supplying much of the cloth that kept their families warm, and the order was met with many howls of protest from various junior officers who had promised the proprietor that the mill would be spared due to its loyalist past. As the mill was put to the torch, many men of the Second and Third Brigades hung their heads, as they knew that their actions were not in the best interest of their cause. This miscarriage of justice, which was remorsefully remembered by many participants, was later revisited when Stoneman officially rebuked Gillem for destroying such a well-known loyalist icon in the region without direct orders.[91]

The confusing and conflicting precedent established at Patterson's Mill was the first unfortunate byproduct of a necessary evil that plagued the raid: the splintering of the chain of command for the benefit of the objective. This fragmentation of the command structure presented a major problem in the execution of the raid, as men were spread too far and thin for George Stoneman to maintain any semblance of direct order. As Stoneman pulled away from Boone, he found it necessary to divide his command in the name of securing forage. The mountains of Southern Appalachia were quickly becoming barren in the upper altitudes, and in order to keep the mounts sufficiently fed to meet the demands of the raid, a wide swath of pillage was carved throughout the region. Stoneman personally led Palmer and the First Brigade to Deep Gap, east of the village, and made for Wilkesboro. The Second and Third Brigades, under Brown and Miller, made for Wilkesboro via the Flat Gap Road, seeking forage in the "Happy Valley" of the Yadkin River.[92]

By the morning of the twenty-ninth, the entire command was on the move, hellbent for Wilkesboro from two separate routes of approach. As they rode through the soupy messes of Flat Gap and Deep Gap Roads, rearguard officers saw fit to arrest every male who did not have a predisposition for the old flag and send them back to Knoxville as a preventative measure against saboteurs. Following the course of the Deep Gap Road, the First Brigade and Stoneman made the roughly thirty-mile ride to the vicinity of Wilkesboro overnight and had established a base of operations by midmorning on the twenty-ninth. As noon approached, elements of the Twelfth Ohio were given the honor of seizing Wilkesboro prior to the First Brigade's anticipated reunion with its sister bodies that evening, both of which were fresh from their fiery conclusion at Patterson's Mill. As the command reorganized and collected stragglers, the Twelfth Ohio swept the town for supplies and suitable mounts to replace the ever-increasing collection of lame animals.[93]

Following the liberation of the Rebel supplies scattered about Wilkesboro—which, tradition holds, contained copious quantities of the white liquor for which the region still achieves notoriety—Palmer's First Brigade began to cross to the north bank of the Yadkin in preparation of advancing into Virginia. For the purpose of securing a toehold on both banks of the swift-flowing river, Palmer ordered his brigade severed in two. The largest wing, consisting of the Tenth Michigan and Fifteenth Pennsylvania under the direct guidance of Palmer, crossed on the evening of the thirtieth, leaving the Twelfth Ohio slated to cross at first light on the morning of March 31. It was on that ill-fated morning along the cold waters of the Yadkin that Stoneman lost his nervously fragile cool, resulting in a temper tantrum of biblical proportions, and staged one of the most memorable impromptu reviews of the entire war.[94]

The first two regiments of Palmer's Brigade crossed quickly and relatively uneventfully; however, the men of the Twelfth Ohio were cursed by the gods of war. As the regiment began to ford the Yadkin, the precipitation from the preceding day's weather began to arrive in full force at this particular juncture in the river. Accounts from survivors claim that the water rose a foot during the hour that it took to expedite the regiment across the river. As

Collecting enough fresh mounts to maintain a steady pace during a protracted raid was one of the most important factors in determining the successful outcome of a campaign. *Courtesy of the Library of Congress.*

The difficulties of crossing non-fordable portions of a river were commonly resented by troopers of both armies. *Courtesy of the Library of Congress.*

the waters intensified, the soggy troopers were left with no other option but swimming their mounts across the Yadkin. While the vast majority of the buoyant pairings made it across the river with little more than a saturated chill to show for it, a few unfortunate equine souls were mired and drowned under the weight of their petrified riders, who refused to distribute the weight of their body off the backs of their mounts and float alongside while holding on to the reins. Although numerous mounts perished, the ultimate loss of the brigade was the drowning of one trooper, who was separated from his mount and swept downriver to a watery demise. The men who successfully forded the Yadkin, in saturated misery, arrived at the feet of General Palmer, who was standing on the veranda of a nice mountain home supervising the disastrous ills befalling his command.[95]

The crossing had been a tragedy of errors. Following the crossing of the Yadkin by all but one member of Palmer's Brigade, Stoneman arrived on site to meet the sole emissary of Palmer's Brigade, Howard A. Buzby, who was left to relay Palmer's intentions to his superior. As Stoneman disembarked, following a short trot from Wilkesboro to the banks of the Yadkin, the supreme commander of the raid was not pleased with the deteriorating situation that confronted him. Haunted by the natural elements during the course of his entire wartime career, Stoneman understood the gravity of his current situation. In the general's mind, a divided army deep within enemy territory was a floundering and exposed command, potentially subjecting his men to the same fate as that of his grand raid in Virginia during the Chancellorsville campaign or his ego-wrenching disaster in central Georgia. Fearing once again that the elements were going to rob him of his hard-fought laurels and possibly send his career into the long-delayed death roll that, up to that point, it had deserved, Stoneman became consumed with anger.[96]

In his twilight years, Howard A. Buzby recalled for the regimental historian that Stoneman and Gillem arrived at the south bank of the Yadkin together. Resting high on their mounts, the pair inquired about the developments surrounding the crossing, the tragic rise in water level and the swiftness of the current. After being the bearer of bad news, the young enlisted man believed that Stoneman had every intention of shooting the messenger and everyone else around him as he spun into a tirade, which the elderly man refused to reenact for the historical record due to the convention of polite conversation. Following the explosive employment of every expletive known to even the most vulgar heathen, the general ordered one of his own staff to swim the river and secure communication with the wayward brigades.[97]

Although the mount on which the trooper sat was renowned for his strength and agility, the natural attributes it possessed did the horse no good against the unencumbered power of the rising river and its increasing current. No sooner had the horse plunged into the water than both rider and mount were in trouble. As Buzby later explained, Stoneman was troubled by the prospect of losing such a fine animal and cursed them both back to safety on the Wilkesboro side of the bank—a feat that was achieved after many arduous attempts to gain a hoof-hold on the south bank. Following their unsuccessful attempt at crossing the river to establish physical communication, Stoneman ordered his staff signalman, Lieutenant Theodore Mallaby, to establish proxy communication with First Brigade signal commander Lieutenant Jerome Rice. With this critical detail taken care of, Stoneman then turned his wrath on his division commander.[98]

While waiting for the signalman on the south bank to prepare his kit and establish discourse with the wayward north bank counterparts, Stoneman turned his attention toward Gillem. The anger that had been brewing inside the New Yorker was all at once turned toward his division commander in a manner that would have led a casual observer to dismiss it as unfair. As his second in command became the current scapegoat, the irate leader of the expedition ordered that he bring the Second and Third Brigades forward for an impromptu parade and inspection. The order was sudden, unexpected and the recipe for the ensuing fiasco.

Amused by the situation, God Almighty contributed to the misery of the south bank partition of Gillem's division by bestowing on it a deluge of biblical proportions. The explosion of inclement weather led Buzby to recall that the saturation thrown upon the division was the principal culprit for its disheveled exterior appearance. Despite the torrential rain and knee-deep mud, it was the shocking condition of Gillem's division, consisting primarily of the "Home Yankees" from Brown's and Miller's Brigades, that resulted in the parade's undoing.

As was consistent with the economy of Appalachia before the war, the populace of the Wilkesboro region was engaged in home distillation to improve its profits from the yearly corn crop. The end result was naturally a high-proof white whiskey that was readily accepted as a medium of exchange for generations. As soldiers who were knowledgeable of local stock moved through the area, these distilleries were actively sought out. Many were hidden in secluded coves due to a recent Confederate moratorium on the distillation of grains undertaken in an effort to maximize food production. As a matter of course, the thirsty enlisted men uncovered the wayward copper icons they sought and soon were smuggling their Appalachian ambrosia within the secure confines of their stomachs.[99]

The unfortunate timing of their consumption coincided with Stoneman's fiery order for a review. This startling call for assembly naturally left many of the men desperately searching for any semblance of sobriety or equilibrium. As the procession advanced along the muddy road before Stoneman and the unfortunate private, who was experiencing his superior's wrath via proxy, the peculiar scene of one of the more memorable cavalcades of the war began to unfold. Many of the troopers in the two brigades were unable to maintain their equilibrium, as the only stimulant that kept them conscious during the parade was the frigid sensation of the rain blasting against their flushed cheeks. Buzby recalled that a number of the casualties resulting from this fiasco could have easily been chalked up for dead, as corn whiskey is a dreadfully potent concoction.[100]

Perhaps the most memorable, or unfortunate, participants in the parade were a number of privates who were chauffeured unconsciously through the procession on commandeered wagons and buggies in plain sight before the fuming general. As Buzby recalled, all the carriages and omnibuses along the

Seasonal distillation, which was commonly practiced along the path of the raid, had been a cultural and economic mainstay in Appalachia for nearly a century. *Courtesy of the Library of Congress.*

With drink readily available to soldiers, the management and punishment of drunken troopers was almost a daily occurrence during the war. *Courtesy of the Library of Congress.*

route had been confiscated. One in particular was a carriage of the George Washington style, filled to the brim with soldiers, with their boots sticking out in all directions. Furthermore, there was a well-known local stagecoach, which had operated between Rutherfordton and the Blue Ridge, filled to the point that the doors barely closed, and its excess baggage consisted of troopers piled on top like cordwood. Buzby further remarked that this unkempt and sobbingly drunken procession stretched for more than a mile.[101]

Naturally, this comical scene only served to promote Stoneman's wrath. As the intoxicated junior officers rode by, Stoneman personally reached out as if trying to strangle them with his powerful hands and berated them in the most ferociously profane manner that the old officer could muster. Following this devilishly emasculating rebuke of his junior officers, Stoneman ordered a halt to the procession and instructed his staff to make camp where they stood—a clear sign that the general was resigned to the wasted condition of his command. Stoneman's tent was erected, and he retired to brood in its privacy after a firm admonishment of his senior officers for their laxity.[102]

Nervously content to communicate through signalmen, Stoneman was informed that there were no Confederate movements detected on the north bank of the Yadkin, and aside from a minor interruption by aggressive bushwhackers on the night of the thirtieth, all had been quiet on Palmer's side of the aquatic obstruction. Cautiously relieved by this welcomed information, Stoneman was resigned to warily operate along both banks of the river, surely with the memories of the previous disasters brought about by natural impediments swimming through his head. Ordering the Second and Third Brigades eastward along the south bank of the river toward Jonesville, the First Brigade was instructed to shadow its counterparts as far as possible and to camp opposite Jonesville the following evening, or as close as the availability of forage would permit.[103]

Advancing down the river, Palmer and the First Brigade displayed remarkable consideration for civilian property. As a local farmer, James Gwyn, recalled, the only burden placed on the local population on the north side of the Yadkin was the liberation of a few livestock, for which cash money was exchanged, and the confiscation of corn to serve as fodder for mounts in spots depleted of natural forage. Another point of interest about Palmer's advance along the north bank of the Yadkin was Gwyn's observation concerning the treatment of opportunistic locals in the face of the Unionist occupation of their valley.[104]

Gwyn noted that the area around Wilkesboro was full of men who had taken every step to pacify the powers that be, no matter what side they

Foraging for fodder was a common duty for trooper and teamster alike. *Courtesy of the Library of Congress.*

belonged to, and the raiders were well aware of this tendency. As Palmer's men rode into the locale, they were greeted by a multitude of locals, who clamored about their strong support for the Union; this boasting merely caused dismay to develop and contempt to boil over among the troopers. Under this climate of dissatisfaction, the only documented looting by Palmer's men was directed at those claiming to be strong Unionists. The movement along the north bank by the First Brigade ranks among the more uneventful actions undertaken by a foraging army in any armed conflict found in the annals of war. Palmer himself even expressed remorse for the little he had to take from a noble secessionist of the Masonic order and prided himself on the fact that he attempted to leave these men of the Yadkin Valley as unmolested as possible.[105]

On the morning of April 1, Stoneman's main body arrived at Jonesville. During the early afternoon hours, Palmer's First Brigade arrived at Elkin, directly across the Yadkin from Jonesville. There, the men were welcomed by the queer sight of women being employed on a factory floor. In the three mills found in Elkin, sixty of the employees were women, whom tradition remembers were exuberantly excited about the arrival of the raiders. It was there that the very same women led the raiders to a storehouse full of enough provisions to last the brigade on the north bank of the Yadkin a few days, including prized stockpiles of molasses, tobacco and seasoned chestnuts.[106]

While many of the enlisted men were enjoying their newfound female admirers—whether opportunist or genuinely Unionist remains to be recorded—the signal detachment under Lieutenant Rice sought out an adequate position in which to reestablish communication with the south bank. About 2:00 p.m., the First Brigade once again opened communication with the remainder of the division. Although the commands were more than relieved to resume their comforting role as mirror images of each other, the river was too swift and high to afford a safe crossing. Thus, Stoneman was forced to continue the dangerous parallel toward the town of Rockford, located on the north bank.[107]

As the split personalities of the division advanced along the Yadkin, the unintended advancement farther east in search of a suitable river crossing brought a new level of angst to the Confederate authorities in North Carolina. Their line of march along the eastern flow of the Yadkin was incidentally directed toward Salisbury, home of one of the last functional supply depots, manufacturing centers and prisoner of war camps under the diminishing control of the Confederacy. This accidental route alarmed the Confederate hierarchy to such an extent that troops were diverted from the delaying action in front of Sherman to protect the precious supply center. Along the western plateau overlooking Salisbury, General Pierre Gustave Toutant de Beauregard fortified positions along the approach to the city with a reinforced brigade of infantry, a move that would have surely jeopardized the success of the raid should Stoneman have elected to seize the critical city from the west.[108]

However, in actuality, the command had no intention of falling upon Salisbury, or at least not at the moment. Instead, Stoneman was anxiously awaiting an opportunity to move the entirety of his command to the north bank of the Yadkin. Once a river crossing was forced, it was the general's intention to move on his primary objective, rendering the East Tennessee and Virginia Railroad near Christiansburg, Virginia, useless. While the wait was excruciating for the veteran New Yorker, the old man was soon to experience a rarity in his wartime experience—a stroke of luck.

Over the next twelve hours, Palmer and the First Brigade secured enough local boats to construct an impromptu ferry crossing and completed the task about 9:00 p.m. on the night of April 1. Stoneman wasted no time, and by midmorning on the second, the majority of the division had forced a successful crossing, aided largely by the subsiding current of the river and a very stout rope ferry fashioned by Palmer's men. Following the reunification of the command, a swift march to the northeast was undertaken as Stoneman advanced his men toward Dobson and Mount Airy. As the raiders traveled the main thoroughfare of Dobson on the afternoon of the second, a few men from the Second Brigade seized the Confederate post office and ransacked the mail for official correspondence. Tragically, all their prying eyes encountered were the heartbreaking echoes of ghosts, whose last testaments would never make it to the eyes and ears of the loved ones they held so dear.[109]

Continuing along the road that wound between Dobson and Mount Airy, the First Brigade overtook a lightly guarded wagon train bound for Christiansburg. Considering the previous consensus of the local Confederate authority that Stoneman was raiding in the direction of Salisbury, the soldiers detailed to the train were no doubt surprised to witness a brigade of Federal cavalry rain down on them along a road that was considered safe. The train was in transit to Christiansburg because Robert E. Lee had already made the decision that the Army of Northern Virginia was to make ready to relocate to a more stable line along the Roanoke River. Naturally, none of the recent decisions made by the Confederate high command was known by the raiders or even the wagoners leading the train.[110]

The supply train, which consisted of anywhere between seventeen and twenty-seven wagons, was overtaken with little more than a few warning shots fired into the air. The lack of resistance on the part of the auxiliary Confederates was an obvious sign that the unescorted muleskinners were no longer engrossed in the level of patriotism that plagues those who are willing to trade their lives for a cause. Following the arrest of the wagons, the imprisonment of its teamsters and the impressments of its mules, the wagons were burned along the roadside near modern-day Dalton. As tradition holds, the spot where the impromptu incineration took place could be identified by the piles of wagon rims hidden in the roadside undergrowth well into the twentieth century.[111]

Aside from the destruction of the supply train, the local inhabitants surrounding Mount Airy were visited by small fragments of the command. One visitation of note was to the home of the retired sideshow anomalies Chang and Eng Bunker, who had settled in the area two decades earlier to raise their families and to cultivate a livelihood in agriculture. The Bunkers, who had two sons serving in the Confederate army, were remiss toward the

This field sketch of a reduced wagon is indicative of the Southern roadways that were left littered with war debris in the wake of marauding armies. *Courtesy of the Library of Congress.*

blue-jacketed curiosity-seekers who arrived on their property, with hats in hand, and largely remained behind closed doors. However, misadventure did not totally avoid the conjoined siblings.[112]

As tradition holds, one company captain had the names of all the local male residents placed into a hat. The names that his subordinate drew were drafted as impressed teamsters and charged with returning some of the captured Confederate wagon trains to Union lines. As the names were craftily selected, a peculiar conundrum arose: Eng was drafted, but Chang avoided the dishonor. The mustering officer beseeched Chang to accompany his brother on the forced expedition, but the ornery right hemisphere of the duo refused to budge on the grounds that he was a moral secessionist. Word was sent of the development to the general staff, and, upon falling on Stoneman's ears, the situation was dismissed out of its sheer ridiculousness. The elderly draftee was allowed to return home with his uncooperative anchor in tow.[113]

Retiring to western North Carolina in order to raise a family in peace, the world-renowned Siamese twins Eng and Chang Bunker are seen here with their respective sons, Patrick Henry and Albert Bunker, both of whom served in the Confederate army. *Courtesy of the North Carolina Collection Photographic Archives, Patrick Henry Bunker, Eng Bunker, Chang Bunker and Albert Bunker Portrait Collection.*

While Stoneman's command had been instrumental in demonstrating to the inhabitants of the mountain coves of Western North Carolina that the war had been soundly decided in the loyalist favor, the general had yet to achieve a single primary objective. However, this withstanding distinction was soon to be remedied as the command made preparations to penetrate Virginia in force. But before the command could pose a threat to the East Tennessee and Virginia Railroad, it had to recover ground lost in its precarious race against the rushing current of the swollen Yadkin. Due to its accidental progress into the eastern extremity of Western North Carolina, the command was forced to once again turn west toward the Blue Ridge and move along the crest at Fancy Gap.[114]

It was there, near the town of Hillsville on April 3, that the command experienced its first armed resistance in days. Knowing that there was Union activity presenting danger to southwest Virginia from a multitude of directions, remnants of the Virginia militia attempted to slow the progress of the raiders by throwing up reinforced barricades at the mouth of the gap. However, the enfeebled old men and blossoming young boys charged with securing the nether reaches of Lee's rear echelon were no match for a division of hardened Union veterans. Carrying on the precedent established by the home guard organizations to the northwest, as Phillip Sheridan came crashing down from the Shenandoah to tighten the noose around the Army of Northern Virginia's neck, the mix-and-match rabble in front of Stoneman dissolved right before his men's eyes after a mild volley of heavy-metal encouragement. By the wee morning hours of April 4, Stoneman's entire command was resting comfortably in and around Hillsville.[115]

While the severely outnumbered and outgunned home guard quickly dissolved without a serious fight, Stoneman's fortunes could have quickly changed due to the ever-growing Confederate presence in southwestern Virginia. Anticipating the collapse of the defensive works around Petersburg and the need to keep every avenue of escape open in the event of necessary exodus, the Confederate hierarchy had begun to shore up the noncombative regions west of Petersburg. Responsibility for security in southwest Virginia was delegated to John Echols, who had approximately five thousand infantry and twenty-two hundred cavalry, most of whom were second-tier soldiers, home guard and junior reserves. Another point of contention that would have had a profound effect on the raid, which incidentally was only known to the Confederate general staff, was that the area that Stoneman's command had been instructed to operate against had been chosen as the rallying point for the Army of Northern Virginia should the long-awaited collapse of the Petersburg line unfold.[116]

Although unable to stop the advance of Stoneman's troopers into his district, John Echols was able to avoid the surrender of his command at both Appomattox and Bennett Place. Later, he would accompany Jefferson Davis on his exodus to Georgia. *Courtesy of the Library of Congress.*

It was at this critical juncture, in the days surrounding April 2, 1865, that events well beyond the control of Stoneman transformed both the definition and objective of the raid. With the Army of Northern Virginia taken to wing, the peaceful, rolling terrain of southwestern Virginia instantly skyrocketed in its strategic value. Having originally been turned loose to destroy transportation infrastructure in southwest Virginia, Stoneman was now in the advantageous position to slow Lee's retreat to the southwest and into the highlands of Western North Carolina. Any delay bestowed on the Army of Northern Virginia by a skirmishing division under Stoneman would allow Grant enough time to close the gap on his prey from the east and force a significant rearguard action that could bring the war to a close in the Eastern Theater.

At this paramount moment in the history of the war, Stoneman was still unaware of the developments around Richmond, as one critical day would pass before the general received a Virginia newspaper from a courier outlining the events on April 4. Encouraged by rumor that the Confederate army was on the move, Stoneman personally amended his directive and took it upon himself to foster a situation that would slow the fleeing

Confederate army a full day before receiving confirmation of its flight. The plan that Stoneman orchestrated while in the saddle on the afternoon of the third greatly fragmented his command into small marauding parties—yet another adaptation of his "bursting shell" doctrine. This time, specific targets were assigned to each fragment, with an emphasis on transportation and communication lines in lieu of the general civilian terrorism that had dominated the preceding week.[117]

It was at this point that the raid expanded from roughly six thousand men moving in two columns to a region-wide infestation of Federal troopers that still haunts the local collective memory. The night of April 3 through the morning of April 4 proved to be a hectic dozen or so hours that witnessed the raiders divided to such an extent that a chronological study of the events that followed became a difficult undertaking. With no fewer than ten separate fragments of the division following the crossing of the Yadkin, the record and memory of the raid muddies. Although their course was confusing, and at times conflicting, they created a historical specter that still haunts Appalachian folklore today. As the raiders moved through the mountainous region, every local tradition fostered a chilling memory in the name of General George Stoneman.

The name in itself became synonymous with the ills that befell the mountains during the waning hours of the war. As a natural progression in the life of local lore, every story passed down through the generations made mention of Stoneman and personally linked him to the thousands of events that occurred throughout the area. This simple dismissal of events following the night of April 3 as the Stoneman Raid is both a great overstatement of the general's role in the campaign and an injustice to the efforts of the increasingly independent subordinate commanders: Miller, Palmer, Brown and Gillem. However, this trend was also a double-edged sword, as Stoneman's name lives on in infamy for the brutality of the later days of the raid, while his subordinate commanders have largely dodged blame for their actions.

Furthermore, the *Official Records of the War of Rebellion* casually dismisses correspondence from the various fragmentations with the unjust moniker of Stoneman's command and mates this gross overstatement with a halfhearted attempt to provide a location of events. The end result is the creation of a monumental task for historians in identifying exactly which regiments were at particular events, who was the commanding officer at certain fiascoes and who exactly was the perpetrator in many local traditions of woe. Despite the hectic nature of studying the multitude of simultaneous actions undertaken by the splintered command, a semblance of chronology does rear its head.

4

"I Believe I'm Talking to the Yankees Now"

W hich side of the car is the door located on, Wickham?" The sentence, barely audible, filled the air as the speeding lieutenant was choked to a gasp by the weight of his accoutrements tightening around his chest and the years of sucking on the teats of countless cigars. This choking sensation, exacerbated by the weight of over thirty pounds clinging to his convulsing body, was heightened under the strain of his first full-speed sprint in recent memory. "I believe it's to my right." The muted words echoed in his ears, projected from the near-distant figure of a lanky man bounding along the crossties directly in front of him. As the middle-aged officer's flabby body struggled to keep time, the private's exclamation was almost lost due to the rush of air howling past his ears.[118]

Staring intently at the back of the private's bobbing head, in much the same way a mule might covet a carrot dangling before his stubborn eyes, the winded officer's brain began to sing with an oxygen-deprived adrenalin rush. "Get to that door and cut that son-of-a-bitch off before he does something to that transmitter," gasped the winded lieutenant. Knowing full well that time was of the essence in this gamble, the pair lunged forward down the rail line toward the switchyard. If they could arrive before the Rebel inhabitants inside the telegraph car became wise to their presence, then their efforts were not in vain.

The race across the mainline and up the course of the spur was executed in earnest by a pair from the Fifteenth Pennsylvania Cavalry. After nearing their target, the frantically scurrying figure in front of the officer leapt over the rails from his bounding path along the crossties and began to run along the course of the southwest side of the freight car. Instinctively, the lieutenant broke to the left, bound for the northeast side of the car, answering a call to the animalistic instinct ingrained in his being, brought on by the desire to trap his prey. Rounding the northeastern side of the car, he could hear the resonation produced by the boots of his subordinate hitting the folding wooden stairs at full speed. The force of each step made the flimsy wood and iron contraption shake, snap and groan.[119]

At this point, the door slid open along its tracks with full force, only to be slammed shut just as suddenly. As the winded private grasped the door handle in an attempt to force his way into the car, his efforts were countered by the inside occupant, who exerted an equal amount of desperate energy to keep the door securely shut. As the struggle unfolded, the iron handle quivered and wrenched in the private's hands as he pulled with all his might—a sure sign that the operator was trying to force the handle into the latch in an effort to lock it. Lieutenant Charles Hinchman ascended the steps in a much calmer, but prudent, manner and reached his arms under Wickman's, searching for any cold iron his fingers could find.[120]

Together, the pair worked counter to the efforts of the operator. With two sets of hands pulling the handle downward and away from the locking mechanism, the door gradually began to give way and commenced the arduous progression along its track. At first, the left foot and shoulder were the only visible parts of the man who was exerting his all to keep the door from being forced ajar. But as the pair of troopers slowly won over, the dark hair smattered with speckles of gray and the cold gray eyes of a man in his early thirties began to emerge from behind the door. It was at that point that Lieutenant Hinchman gave his first bluffing ultimatum: "You let go of this God-damned door, or so help me God I will shoot you where you stand!"[121]

For a moment, it appeared as if the bluff had no effect on the Rebel operator, as the operator continued to battle the pair for the destiny of the door, tooth and nail. However, after a few more seconds of frantic tug of war, it abruptly ceased. The counter pressure on the door was lifted instantly, and the door slid open under the full force of the troopers. This unheralded cessation of the contest sent the unsuspecting lieutenant tumbling from the stairs and into the mud. The door may have been wide open, but the lieutenant was furious at the deceitful audacity of the operator.

As he rose from the muck and ascended the folding stairs into the car, the lieutenant was welcomed by the expected sight of Private Wickman, leveling his carbine at the operator, whose arms were stretched to their fullest vertical limits. As the lieutenant set his right foot into the car and pushed the remainder of his body into it, an unexpected abnormality garnered the attention of his left peripheral—his saber had folded when he fell. The discovery of the thirty-five-degree bend in the lower extremes of his scabbard took his attention away from the task at hand for a few seconds. Attempting to draw the blade in an experiment as to its functionality, an expected result was returned: stuck in the scabbard, a commonly fatal flaw experienced with the army's new light saber. "Damn-it, now I'm going to have to saw it down and re-hone it. There goes today's nap," the bruised officer quietly lamented to himself.[122]

Now, with the lieutenant's rage at a full boil, he reached down with his right arm and unfastened his holster. Drawing his sidearm, he quickly swung it up to mid-chest height, cocked the hammer once into the load position and, with his left hand, spun the cylinder. Taking his eyes off his prize for one instant, he looked down at his Colt, half expecting to see that his fall had clogged the barrel and all six cylinders with mud. It had not. Drawing the hammer back to the firing position, the infuriated officer bent his arm into a relaxed position, pointed the pistol at the operator and instructed him to have a seat at his desk.[123]

Wasting no time, the lieutenant explained the purpose behind their abrupt dissent, a message that was no doubt lost under the constantly reiterated flood of pleas not to fire. Apathetically, the lieutenant disregarded the sheer terror of the operator and began to bark orders at him as if the man were a mongrel dog. Closing in with a strong, determined step, the lieutenant approached to whispering distance before he let loose a deep-baritone demand, "What you're going to do, boy, is open a line with Lynchburg, understand?" The operator, still petrified, only stared at the muzzles of the Colt revolver and Spencer repeater leveled at his chest. Only the reiteration of his inquiry in a louder and more domineering tone brought the operator away from the verge of shock. Collapsing into the sniveling pleas of submissive helplessness, the operator said meekly, "Yes sir, please don't shoot me. I have a wife."

Hinchman instantly interrupted the operator. "Don't even start with that shit. Just follow my instructions to the letter, and you will be let loose in a few minutes."[124]

Understanding the helplessness of his condition, the operator turned toward the desk and transmitter. The rhythmic shaking of his hand made it difficult to open the ledger and ready a pencil. After a few deep breaths, the petrified operator steadied his nerves, located the codebook and opened it to the pages he would need to begin an unsolicited conversation on a government wire. The whole time, his mind was running rampant with a butchered rendition of the Lord's Prayer, his panic-induced piousness rearranging whole verses, adding words and leaving entire mainstays out. Finally, after running the course of a silent prayer through his mind, he moved the current lever on the apparatus to the on position, touched juice to the coil and opened a line with Lynchburg.

While the operator was making his preparations posthaste, the jittery master of the pulsating language was unaware that Hinchman had ordered the private to lower his rifle and supervise the actions of their captive. The private in question, John J. Wickham, held a position of prominence as the regiment's telegraph operator, a post that had left him absent from much of the warm action the regiment had seen in the preceding years. Surveying the executions of the Rebel operator, Wickham was keeping a watchful eye for any irregularity that might tip off Lynchburg as to the true intention of the Rebel operator. Content to stand aside and let his subordinate apply his avocation, the lieutenant simply leveled his pistol directly at the back of the frightened operator and watched with rage-induced curiosity.[125]

As the operator's fingers began to dance with transitive repetition upon the apparatus, sweat began to cascade from his brow. After a few moments of waiting, an acknowledgement pulsed in from the Lynchburg end of the line. "Ask them if they have any word on troop movements in the area, Federal or Confederate," the lieutenant bellowed. Following the completion of his latest request, a long pause was interrupted by the desired signals. For a few silent moments, the operator scribbled silently in his ledger, looking up occasionally to cross-reference his codebook.[126]

After proofreading his deciphering, the operator looked at the gruff officer and told him the most expected news, "He says that Federal cavalry has been reported along the Roanoke River and as far southwest as the Yadkin in North Carolina." Taking a sigh to slow his heart rate, the quivering man continued, "Furthermore, it is rumored that George H. Thomas is advancing east out of the Blue Ridge. It also looks as if the majority of local home guard, militias and regular regiments are assembling in Lynchburg." While it was no surprise that word of the command's actions would have made it as far east as Lynchburg, the lieutenant and the private were both pleasantly surprised to hear that the Confederate intelligence was faulty enough to believe that their division of six thousand men could be mistaken for the entire Army of the Cumberland.[127]

For a moment, the lieutenant thought that the operator was finished, until he piped up with some most unexpected news. In the mouselike whimper of one who knows that he is doing wrong, the operator uttered, "Lynchburg also says that Richmond has been abandoned, and the lines at Petersburg have been breached." After another long pause, he continued, "The army escaped, but the Lynchburg end says that preparations are being made to move Lee and his men in this direction, most likely to Lynchburg."[128]

The news came crashing down on the pair of troopers like a ton of bricks. The end of the war was at hand. Furthermore, the path of destruction chosen for the command ran right through Lee's anticipated line of retreat and essentially trapped the Rebel army. Processing the information, Lieutenant Hinchman mused, "If the Army of the Potomac keeps up the pursuit, then Lee will have to fight, and the Rebel army doesn't have any open rails ahead of them." Completing his calculation of the events at hand, he drifted into fanciful thought. "It's over; it's finally over."

Barely able to contain the smile that was cracking his glower, the lieutenant asked the operator to extract more information. "I want specifics, roads, the size of the army, what generals are with him, where is Jefferson Davis and how long ago did this occur?" Knowing full well that the more information these Yankee raiders had, the more dangerous they were to the cause, the operator sent a request for the specifics but augmented his message with an element of unseen sabotage. As the regiment's telegraph operator looked away to enjoy a few moments reprieve with his commanding officer, the Confederate demonstrated silent bravado. Continuing to send the messages in full, the operator switched over to an amateurish interpretation of the code that bordered on gibberish—certainly not the signature that other operators had come to expect from him.

The silent efforts of the saboteur netted the desired fruits, as the bombardment of questions and emphasis on certain words roused the suspicion of the Lynchburg operator. For several minutes, there was no response from the other end of the line. Then, all at once, a flood of pulses sparked down the line. After tallying them on his ledger and cross-referencing them with his codebook, the operator placed his pencil in his mouth and bit down, half expecting to be knocked in the back of the head by the butt of the officer's pistol. There, in black and white on the tablet, read the following message: "I believe I am talking to the Yankees now."[129]

Following this, a few pulses that were commonly known to spell out expletives began filtering from the line, and then there was nothing. The line had been closed and the conversation terminated. As the two men left the operator at his table, without so much as interrogation, thanks or admonishment, they descended the stairs to the tacks. As the pair began to jog back to their mounts, they were filled with the queer sensation of knowing that, with any luck, the war would be over within a few days. After swinging back into the saddle and heading off to inform their commanding officer of the developments, the pair began to contemplate their morning's work.

Having just learned the fluidity of the Rebel situation in one of the more peculiar telegraph conversations of the war, Lieutenant Hinchman pondered just how widespread the news of Lee's collapse was. Guiding his mount back to the main thoroughfare, he began to think of the swarms of deserters and civilian refugees they would no doubt come across in the ensuing days. It was at that point that his mind drifted to the other elements of the command that were spread across God's creation, and he wondered if they were sharing similar experiences in their enlightenment on the news of the fall of Richmond.

As the piecemeal fragmentations began to take form on paper, Stoneman's main body spent a few precious hours resting at Hillsville, Virginia. Following their intensely deep slumber, no doubt the same rushed sleep experienced by night owls who retire in the still hours of the late night and anxiously loath their impending dawn awakening, the troopers were roused and ordered to resume the march. By the time the morning light was bursting from the eastern horizon, the chronically exhausted troopers were forced back into the saddle and resumed their marathon pace. A few moments before noon, on April 4, the command found itself nearing the tiny hamlet of Jacksonville.[130]

Waiting at the outskirts of the community were two local officials hoisting a white strip of cloth on a skinned tree branch; the middle-class cross-section consisting of a doctor and a lawyer stood on weak knees to declare the town an open community. The town's decision to greet the raiders under a flag of truce, a tactic employed by countless communities at this juncture in the war, was undertaken out of fear that the hamlet would be put to the torch due to the misconception that the community was openly secessionist. Much to the village's relief, the command did not set the town afire. Instead, the weary troopers were content to rest their mounts near an ample stockpile of hay.[131]

The first fragment of Stoneman's command to be amputated from the main body was a sizable portion of the Third Brigade. Outside Hillsville, Colonel John Miller was ordered to handpick five hundred able riders and advance on to Wytheville via Potter's Ford. It goes without saying that the order did not come as welcomed news, as April 4 was just a few moments old, and the men in question had yet to receive a moment's rest that night. Once underway, Miller was instructed to pass through Wytheville and render the railroad trestles that spanned Reedy Creek useless to the enemy. A particular prize of interest to Stoneman was the largest of the trestles located at Max Meadows. Furthermore, he was under orders to void Wytheville of any provisions that the renegade army might find useful and to burn any advantageous infrastructure not brought to their attention by Federal intelligence.[132]

The Tennesseans Miller chose for the operation, men whose families had experienced years of hardship at the hand of the Confederate forces in the mountains, were chomping at the bit for a chance to extract a little revenge on their secessionist counterparts in Virginia. They were not to be disappointed, as outside Wytheville, Miller's men were engaged in the first hotly contested action of the raid. Elements of Confederate general John C. Vaughn's cavalry collided with the advance guard of the fragment about midmorning on the fourth. The engagement was hot, quick, deadly and wholly confusing as the events that transpired during the flash firefight were greatly contradicted in the correspondence of both sides.[133]

From the Union perspective, Miller recalled that his men had repulsed an inaugural charge by Vaughn and drove a secondary line from the field at the expense of thirty-five casualties given up by the Confederates. In addition to his scant description of the entanglement, no effort was given toward identifying what form his own casualties took. On the other hand, Vaughn reported to his superiors that he had successfully drawn the approaching force into an ambush, and his successful skirmishing resulted in forcing the Federal troopers to divert their line of march away from their intended objective. Unfortunately, Confederate records were mute on the issue of casualties accumulated by Vaughn during the scrape.[134]

Although the course of the engagement is debated, the outcome is certain. Following the clash, Miller's detachment moved through Wytheville without incident and collected an unrecorded number of stores. After completing its business in town, the fragment cautiously advanced to the banks of Reedy Creek and established a base camp. There, Miller posted sentry details in the event that Vaughn made another attempt to rout his detachment, while the bulk of his men set out to complete their assigned task.[135]

As the six bridges that spanned the creek wavered under the onslaught of flames, Miller advanced on an easterly route, knowing that the swift completion of his primary objective afforded him a few hours of marauding. Aware that the jewel of foothills Virginia—Lynchburg—was just a matter of miles away, Miller elected to demonstrate his force in its vicinity. While not attempting an assault on a city that would surely be protected with more than his scant force of about five hundred, his feint toward Lynchburg climaxed four miles from the city limits sign—the easternmost advance by the raiders in Virginia. Satisfied with placing his toe in the unfamiliar waters of west-central Virginia, he reassembled his detachment and then moved to rejoin the remainder of the command.[136]

Another notable partition of Stoneman's command was a collection of 250 handpicked men from the Fifteenth Pennsylvania Cavalry under Major William Wagner. Their orders were to advance toward the vicinity of Salem, Virginia, and destroy any railroad infrastructure that the troopers could lay their hands on. Following the successful completion of his primary objective, Wagner was instructed to advance to the easternmost point that the Confederates would yield without forcing a general engagement and to strike at targets of opportunity before returning to the main body. Turned loose on a rolling countryside, the Fifteenth Pennsylvania rode hard, and the detachment reached Christiansburg in the early daylight hours of the fifth.[137]

The raiders advanced toward the town at such a rapid pace that the local population had little warning of their presence. Unlike other surprise visits to Southern boroughs by Federal raiders, the men of the Fifteenth Pennsylvania were not welcomed by the loathsome sight of local notables brandishing a white flag—a sight that had occurred with increasing regularity at the outskirts of hamlets that lay in Stoneman's path. As the troopers stormed along the main thoroughfare, startled civilians made for any avenue of possible escape. As was to be expected, the troopers rounded up a large number of local noncombatants and began an impromptu interrogation. Upon prodding a few individuals, it was revealed to the inquisitors that an active Confederate telegraph office was located within the town, housed in a railroad car that rested on the eastern outskirts. It was in this isolated

With the telegraph and rail recent introductions to North American warfare, the combination of the two aided in the unprecedented intelligence boom that occurred during the war. *Courtesy of the Library of Congress.*

car that an unsuspecting Confederate operator was introduced to the likes of Lieutenant Charles S. Hinchman and Private John J. Wickham—a less than cordial meeting that opened the Fifteenth Pennsylvania's eyes to the developments farther east.[138]

Following the comically fruitful debacle in Christiansburg, the fragment followed the course of the Bent Mountain Road and arrived at the village of Salem during the early afternoon hours. Upon arrival, the detachment was disheartened to discover that the valuable Confederate stores, which had been housed in the town for several days, had departed via rail just five minutes earlier. Eager to achieve one of his stated objectives, Wagner sent a detachment to pursue the locomotive in anticipation of overtaking it. While a fraction of his men began their pursuit of the iron horse, the few wagons in town abandoned by the Rebel government were taken to one end of town and burned.[139]

Farther down the line at Conyers' Station, the fugitive train was captured as it stopped to refuel and load further supplies. While the train was composed of a solitary freight car, engine and wood box, it was loaded to the hilt with a sizeable chunk of the Confederacy's last crop of tobacco. Naturally, the men of the detachment helped themselves to the booty and commenced to set enough aside to pacify the appetites of their absent comrades. Following the partition of the Rebel stores, the remaining sundries were turned over to a small collection of self-emancipated blacks, who had arrived in short order as rumor spread throughout the area that Federal troopers were converging at the junction. The tobacco was distributed among the motley crew, which had every intention of following the troopers as closely as possible to avoid the rampant home guard presence in the region. Concerned that a cavalcade of renegade slaves might slow the progress of the detachment, the raiders expedited the incineration of the train and promptly returned to Wagner's main body.[140]

After the fragment reunited, Wagner advanced his men onto Buford's farm near the Peak of Otter about ten o'clock on the night of the fifth and bivouacked in a pasture for the remainder of the evening. Tradition holds that the proprietor of the farm, Buford, was an elderly man who had relatives engaged as combatants on both sides of the conflict. Because of this family division, the old man had tried to maintain as neutral a stance as the war would afford him. In an extension of his good will, Buford opened his barn to the raiders for forage and even demanded that the officers have breakfast at his table in the morning—a request that needed no reconsideration, given that it was the first sit-down meal offered to the officers in roughly two weeks.[141]

The following morning, April 6, the fragment pushed onward. Impressed by the unusual amount of hospitality and cordialness that Buford demonstrated at breakfast, Wagner returned the air of brotherhood by leaving Buford's farm unmolested, going so far as to not pilfer a single unoffered ear of corn from his crib as the fragment departed for Liberty, Virginia. It was there, on the outskirts of town, that the raiders encountered the expected norm for southwest Virginia—the town's mayor wielding metaphorical sovereignty on a stick. Without incident, the advantageous politician surrendered the town as an open community to the raiders, which was directly followed by pleas for the uneventful passage of the aggressors through the quaint little village. Pressed for time, the raiders were more than happy to oblige, as not a single raider even went so far as to dismount within the confines of the community.[142]

The reason for the unusual expediency through Liberty was that Wagner's primary objectives had yet to be reached. Within sight of the Big and Little Otter Rivers, the fragment separated into lesser detachments and made for the bridges that spanned the swift waters. It was there that Major Wagner began to have a crisis of faith. With the newfound information that Lee was dislodged from his nearly yearlong siege and the prospect of the war's conclusion looming, the major began to question the strategic purpose of his mission. If the war was rapidly winding down, then why partake in the pointless destruction of infrastructure that would greatly aid the local population once they have been assimilated?[143]

As a man who appreciated aesthetic construction, the twin bridges across the Big and Little Otter Rivers were a sight to behold. According

The bridge and trestle over Platt Creek in East Tennessee are typical of common construction techniques seen during the war. The trestle had witnessed previous sabotage, and makeshift repairs are evident. *Courtesy of the Library of Congress.*

to Wagner's description, the trestle across the senior-most creek was of the covered variety, measuring approximately 600 feet long and 100 feet tall. Its awe-inspiring wooden construction splendidly fit the tranquil valley in which it resided, presenting almost an air of serenity from the cliff side overlooking it. The trestle over the Little Otter was identical in design but larger in scale, as the colossus was constructed to be 900 feet long and 150 feet high. Their architectural beauty tripped up Wagner, who instantly began to admire the pair as testaments to local engineering, leading him to the decision that the bridges needed to be preserved for future generations.[144]

Thoroughly convinced of the potential postwar importance that the structures possessed, Major Wagner instructed his men to gather dry deadfall and fence rails from the surrounding countryside in order to construct pyres at the base of the trestles. However, the scavengers were strictly forbidden to proceed any farther until he had personally given the order to light the pyres. While his men constructed the instruments of the structures' undoing, Wagner suspended further action in anticipation of the arrival of revised instructions from either Palmer or Stoneman. The detachment was ordered to bivouac, and Wagner anxiously held out hope that a courier would arrive with orders to cease the operation.[145]

For Wagner, the morning of the seventh was filled with the nervous tension that swiftly erodes a stomach lining into a haggard hive of ulcers. Staring down the road for any sign of communication from a superior officer occupied the entire afternoon and most of the evening. Finally, disheartened that he could no longer, in good conscience, wait for any word from his disjointed superiors, Wagner ordered his men to put the trestles to the torch at 11:00 p.m. As the tinder combusted, it surely created a beautifully disheartening sight while the flames consumed the trestles and licked at the night sky in a spectacular inferno.[146]

Following the unfortunately successful destruction of the covered trestles, the fragment proceeded to leave the banks of the Big and Little Otter Rivers during the early morning hours of the eighth. Like the fragment under Miller's command, Wagner advanced along an easterly route, flirting with the town of Lynchburg. It was along that muddy road that Wagner's fragment received its first taste of the growing Confederate presence in the area. As a squad serving as the advance guard had broken through the tree line into a clearing, the air became saturated with lead loosed by a thinly dispersed Confederate picket line.[147]

Roughly ten miles southwest of the city, the Confederate volley startled the unsuspecting Federal cavalry, which in turn withdrew back to the safety

Typically, bridges and trestles were rendered useless by starting a fire around the weaker wooden pylons. The end result was a collapsed center span that took several days to repair. *Courtesy of the Library of Congress.*

of the tree line, dismounted and then advanced in skirmish formation. The Union skirmishers exchanged fire with the Confederate pickets until the latter were ordered to withdraw to a more sustainable defensive position. Cautiously advancing and expecting a renewal of the bloodless scrape at any moment, Wagner halted his men to rest six miles from the outskirts of the city. While the bulk of the fragment anxiously rested, a section of eight men under Corporal Vance Gilmore was detached for a scouting detail.[148]

Gilmore was ordered to take his squad and advance slowly in the direction of Lynchburg in an attempt to gather as much intelligence as his precarious situation would allow. The small splinter of men exercised a profound level of caution, distributing their numbers equally along the edges of the road and avoiding the open expanse at the middle of the road with somber peculiarity, as if creating a solitary hoof print in the muddy median spelled certain death. The advance of the troopers was tedious, as the majority of their expedition was undertaken from a dismounted position. Gilmore elected that the safest option was to slowly crawl toward Lynchburg along improvised footpaths, which would safely lead his squad around suspected ambush points and picket outposts.

After arriving within earshot of Lynchburg, the squad had seen and heard all that troopers needed in order to grasp the solemnity of the entire battalion's situation. It was at that point that Gilmore reversed his men's course and made for the relative safety of Wagner's position. The scouting detail returned with the information that Wagner had suspected all along. As Gilmore best surmised, a sizeable collection of Confederate forces of unknown origins was occupying the city. This concentration of Rebel forces made any advancement by the battalion an exercise in futility. Wagner, pacified that all of his primary objectives had been accomplished, opted not to press his luck and ordered his men to ride to the west in an effort to rejoin the Fifteenth Regiment and Palmer's Brigade.[149]

The return trip was slow going, as Wagner had to rely on information extracted from locals in order to make a valid estimate where the rendezvous with Palmer's Brigade might occur. After riding blindly throughout most of the day on the ninth, Wagner's battalion bivouacked along the roadside and then made for Henry Courthouse the following morning. At the outskirts of town, the fragment halted to allow time for their mounts to take fodder. In the midst of their short reprieve, the troopers were approached by a family of local Tories.[150]

These friendly bearers of bad news let it be known that a Confederate brigade of about fifteen hundred infantry, freshly arrived from Danville, was waiting up the road at the courthouse. The soldiers had been dispatched to the town with the intention of halting the various raids in the Army of Northern Virginia's rear. Furthermore, it had been made abundantly clear that the commander of the brigade was well aware of the battalion's presence on the road leading into town.[151]

Fearful of detection, Wagner moved his men out of the pasture and into the tree line. From that point on, noise discipline was imposed on the small battalion, and the men nervously waited for darkness to encompass the landscape. That evening, Wagner ordered his men to mount up quietly, not to smoke or light a single match, to abstain from talking with the exception of anyone over the rank of sergeant and to hold on to their sabers to prevent unwanted clanking as the blades rattled inside their metallic sheaths. In the blinding dark, Wagner commenced his march to the southwest of Henry Courthouse. Utilizing narrow side roads and pasture paths outlined by sympathetic locals, the battalion avoided unwanted attention from the Confederate force.[152]

Knowing that time was of the essence, Wagner drove his men hard all through the night and most of the following day. Stopping only long enough to rest their mounts and to inspect suspicious landscapes brought to their attention by their growing paranoia over the threat of ambush, the fragment spent the better part of eighteen hours in the saddle. The battalion, delirious for want of sleep, eventually made contact with a foraging party detached from the First

Brigade, just a few miles northeast of the main body, on the late afternoon of the eleventh. By the time the night had ended, Wagner was debriefing Palmer on the accomplishments of his fragment, the presence of increased troop levels near Henry Courthouse, events surrounding the fall of Petersburg and what little was known about the movements of the Army of Northern Virginia.[153]

The journey of Wagner's fragment of the Fifteenth Pennsylvania had been Homeric in scale. Leaving Christiansburg on April 5, the men had traveled 288 miles in six days. During the course of their expedition, Wagner's men had obtained concrete proof of the fall of the Virginia Gibraltar, as Lee's army was once again traversing the open spaces; achieved their primary objective after much faltering resignation; engaged the enemy successfully without the loss of a single trooper; and avoided detection by two large forces dispatched by the Confederate authorities to pursue them. Furthermore, the raiders had captured and paroled several dozen Confederate deserters along the way. Throughout all of this, the fragment had conducted itself as the shining example of the gentleman soldier—a rare and hard-to-master feat in the confusing closing days of a very gruesome conflict.[154]

While elements of the Fifteenth Pennsylvania and Miller's Brigade were destructively gallivanting in the vicinity of Lynchburg, other splinters from various brigades undertook operations of equal importance. Detachments from the Second Brigade, most notably those from the Eleventh Kentucky, were sent to obstruct rail navigation through the New River Valley. Like the other fragments of the command, the Kentuckians struck out of Christiansburg on the morning of April 5, riding the majority of the night and most of the following morning without respite to reach their distant destination. The Eleventh Kentucky Cavalry, by far one of the more sizeable of the fragments unleashed by Stoneman, was diligent in its work and did an immeasurable amount of damage to vital Confederate infrastructure.[155]

Arriving along the rail link that dissected the valley about midmorning on the sixth, the regiment was divided into work details and spread throughout the vicinity. The men of the Bluegrass State proved extremely diligent despoilers, as they tore loose iron rails and uprooted crossties in pre-assigned subsections. While the tracks were assaulted by one portion of the regiment, smaller detachments busied themselves with gathering enough tinder to build fires suitable to incinerate the various trestles that spanned the New River. Racing against the clock, the men pushed themselves to the limits of their endurance. Exhausted, the troopers were rewarded for their efforts by being ordered to return to Christiansburg without rest, and eventually the regiment rejoined the command by midafternoon on the seventh.[156]

The destruction of communication and transportation lines, such as the widespread destruction undertaken by the Eleventh Kentucky, was a multifaceted task that hinged on solid communication among many fragments. *Courtesy of the Library of Congress.*

In the end, their work was swift and highly effective. It was noted in the official report that by four o'clock on the afternoon of the sixth, all the bridges over the New River were engulfed in flames. Moreover, the majority of the rails and crossties had been rendered useless for twenty miles beyond the easternmost trestles. It was perhaps the most destructive six hours of the entire raid and still stands as a testament to the abilities of a regiment's worth of motivated mounted men.[157]

Along with Palmer's dissection of the Fifteenth Pennsylvania under Major Wagner, the Quaker general also fragmented his First Brigade by sending the entire Tenth Michigan Cavalry along the Roanoke River to render the bridges untenable. Although traveling through an area hostile to its presence, this large concentration of blue uniforms was met with little resistance. Similar to the efforts of the Second Brigade undertaken by the Eleventh Kentucky, the Tenth Michigan divided the work amongst details in order to expedite its task. Its efforts were successful, and by the early evening hours of the sixth, the bridges were reduced to smoldering embers, and the regiment was well on its way toward a reunion with its comrades in arms long before the Confederates could muster a force to stop it.[158]

With roughly half of his troopers committed to ventures that made this incarnation of the "bursting shell" a resounding success, Palmer was instructed to utilize the remainder of his command in further attacks on

Confederate infrastructure. About midafternoon on the fifth, Stoneman instructed Palmer to render the railroad east of Christiansburg useless. As the remnants of the Fifteenth Pennsylvania and the Twelfth Ohio began to undertake their prescribed task, they were fortunate enough to labor uninterrupted over the course of two days. The diligence that the two regiments devoted to their assignment rivaled the best efforts of Sherman's men in central Georgia on their march to the sea. All together, the activities of the First and Second Brigades effectively destroyed the East Tennessee and Virginia Railroad on both the eastern and western boundaries of Christiansburg—an achievement that isolated most of southwest Virginia from the dying Confederate government.[159]

In all, the various fragments were highly effective against the remaining Confederate rail infrastructure. Approximately one hundred miles of rail were rendered useless, including no fewer than a dozen bridges and trestles put to the torch. Furthermore, as the command moved through the area, it gathered a large collection of the bonded searching for a personal exodus. Not overlooking an opportunity to utilize their services, these men and women were put to work as impromptu contraband followers at Christiansburg, where they labored away at cooking fry bread and preparing rations for the raiders.[160]

However, the rapid pace of the preceding day's actions took its effect on the equipment and mounts of the raiders. The remaining ambulances were disabled due to the muddy roads, forcing Stoneman to cautiously leave his wounded and dead with paroled Confederate doctors at captured hospitals. His mounts were tired, and an idle pace was implemented over the course of the next two days for the majority of the command. This reprieve not only allowed time for the mounts to consume ample amounts of fodder and for troopers to replace their lame horses from the growing collection of acceptable specimens collected along their line of march, but it also allowed time for the absent fragments under Miller and Wagner to reunite with the command.[161]

As the command initiated its return march to North Carolina, leading the Tarheels to lament their premature sigh of relief following Stoneman's entrance into Virginia, the raiders were surely unaware of the substantial effect their actions had on the conclusion of the war. While their role in the surrender at Appomattox was that of accidental vicariousness, the location of the raiders and a lack of Confederate intelligence greatly affected Lee's understanding of the scope of his encirclement. With reports of large cavalry demonstrations ahead of his line of march, Lee could only suspect the worst from the reports pouring out of southwestern Virginia. Of all the actions undertaken by

Stoneman's final "bursting shell" that were brought to Lee's attention, the riders under Wagner and Miller worried the aging general the most.[162]

Knowing of their joint ventures around the western extremes of Lynchburg, Lee's only avenue of retreat following Sheridan's victory at Saylor's Creek and George Armstrong Custer's flanking of the Army of Northern Virginia at Appomattox Station, the Confederate commander was under a false assumption that Lynchburg was soon to be overtaken by a large force under George H. Thomas that had crossed over the mountains. However, Thomas had made no such attempt to corner the fleeing army. The misinformation presented to him by his scouts led the tired general to believe that his situation was hopeless. Following a halfhearted breakout attempt by the remaining armed men of the army under John B. Gordon on April 9, Lee sent a dispatch rider from his lines at three o'clock that afternoon, armed with nothing more than an off-colored huck towel and the news that the Army of Northern Virginia intended to surrender.[163]

While some historians have argued that the raid created the illusion of a four-sided encirclement of Lee's army, in reality, the Confederates were only confronted with a Federal presence on three sides. However, the situation was utterly hopeless due to the destruction of the railway lines west of his only avenue of escape—Lynchburg. Had Lee committed his army at Appomattox Court House and miraculously broken through Custer's lines to Lynchburg, the accomplishment would have been in vain. The truth of the matter was that Stoneman had castrated Lee's last remaining option; the rail line that the New Yorker's former commander needed to expedite his evacuation to the Roanoke River was no longer in operation.

As Stoneman's men neared the North Carolina border, they could rightfully share in the satisfaction of Appomattox, although the raiders did not yet know of the development. Through his southwestern Virginia adventure, Stoneman had repaired his reputation as a competent field commander by demonstrating that he could lead a command into the field without infantry and garner highly effective results. The long-awaited successful execution of the "bursting shell" demonstrated that mass chaos created by a decentralized division of cavalry in the rear echelons of enemy territory could benefit a larger infantry operation, precisely as he had long insisted. As Stoneman led his command into North Carolina, he set his eyes on the objectives to which he had aspired since the summer of 1863: the liberation of a rear-echelon enemy prison camp and the elevation of his status to that of cavalry legend.

5

"If We Are Working Hard, We Are Living Well"

I hope that Wagner has the good sense to follow our trail." The repetitive creak of his saddle, the result of the sharp jostle created by his trotting mount, seemed to only encourage Palmer's worrisome contemplation about the whereabouts of his wayward battalion. As the ominous metronome espoused its mocking meter, the ulcer-ridden general lamented his situation in a cyclical fashion that would have easily matched the meditative efforts of the most devout monk from the Far East. "Hell, we are so spread out across the countryside that even a blind mongoloid could find at least one of my riders." This nervous attempt at constant reassurance did the commander of the First Brigade no good. In his mind, an entire battalion had been absent entirely too long, and dangerous amounts of distance were accumulating among his fragmented men. There was no comfort in the fact that it was already midafternoon on April 7 and his brigade had been ordered to move beyond the town of Martinsville in order to secure supplies as the entire command made preparations to reenter North Carolina.[164]

The bulk of the Tenth Michigan was the only force that he had directly under thumb, and Palmer was haunted by the distinct possibility that his under-strength brigade would not be able to withstand an ambush by or direct confrontation with the large bands of Confederate cavalry that had slipped the noose Grant was placing around Lee's neck. "These men are desperate," he thought. "They will fight if cornered." He continued his mental flagellation: "I should not have dived my men along different roads; damn this lack of grass, I need my regiment here for strength."[165]

Passing surprisingly close to Henry Courthouse, ironically the same venue where Wagner's men would avoid detection by a larger Confederate force and pick up the trail of the First Brigade just a few days later, the column snaked its way through Henry County. The countryside was pleasant on this early spring afternoon, and the pace of the riders slowed to a crawl in order to make the journey into North Carolina less burdensome for their fatigued mounts. As the troopers advanced through the rolling hillsides, the church spires at Martinsville could be seen just above the treetops, signifying that their objective was within sight. However, a peculiarity caught the attention of Palmer's advance guard that would bring all his fears to fruition.[166]

While riding amidst the column, Palmer noticed that the procession had slowed to a halt. Lurching forward with his staff, he could see the lieutenant designated to lead the advance guard talking to one of the company commanders. Placing spurs to his mount, the general arrived mid-conversation. "Captain, my scouts tell me that there is a suspicious amount of activity going on in Martinsville," the lieutenant reported with a look of concern creeping over his face. The speculative officer internally dismissed what his scouts had told him as a case of war nerves. When pressed by the captain to explain the rationale for halting the column, he replied, "Smoke, sir. There seems to be a number of open fires in the vicinity of the town, and I'm told that they are too fanned out to be rising from chimneys." Continuing as the spokesman for his men's suspicions, he said, "My men have not heard anything out of the ordinary, but they believe that there is a Rebel encampment in or around the town."

Feeling a lump swell in his throat, Palmer quickly instructed the company commander to shake his men out of the column and cautiously advance as close to Martinsville as they could without being detected, or worse, forcing an engagement. "You find out just how many are in there, which command they belong to, and get your ass back here." Utilizing the delay afforded by a contemplative sigh, he added, "I don't want to start a general row with half of the Rebel cavalry." Turning his mount clear of the road, Palmer watched as the lead company split its detachment into equal partitions along the edges of the road and began to trot off in the direction of the town. As his men rode down the hillside, across a pasture and into the tree line, the Delawarean could only wish for the best while he expected the worst.[167]

After the better part of a half hour, a rider crested the tree line at a full gallop. Riding with his staff to meet the messenger, Palmer received his first information about the mysterious situation that confronted him. "Sir, it's a regiment of cavalry," gasped the dispatch rider, who had obviously been winded by the shock of riding across a rocky field at full speed. "The captain said that he is not entirely sure what command they are attached to, but they are certainly not a part of the Army of Northern Virginia," the corporal affirmed with some degree of authority. Puzzled by this mysteriously unassigned regiment, Palmer pressed for details. "Well, what leads the captain to that assumption, Corporal?"

Realizing that he would have to defend his commander's hypothesis, the corporal caught his breath and explained, "For starters, General, the flag that they have next to their headquarters lean-to is most likely from another army—it's that blue-and-white pattern which we saw in Georgia." This unexpected bit of information took Palmer aback somewhat. He knew full well that Johnston's army was being herded through North Carolina, but to have elements reaching Virginia was incredibly unexpected news. Coming to the realization that he was most likely confronted with a distant foraging party, Palmer pressed the issue. "What else has the captain made mention of about the regiment?"

With all of his dictated instruction spent, the corporal chided, "That's it, General, but if you ask me, these men do not look like they just spent eight months dug in around a supply depot." He added, "They are some of the most unkempt and undisciplined cavalry I have seen in the whole war. Hell, they did not even put out sentries, we literally have the whole company on a picket line less than five hundred yards away from them—they are oblivious." He proudly finished his statement: "For a moment, until the captain got a good look at them with his glasses, most of the boys thought they were home guard or even deserters."

Dismissing the corporal with instructions to hold the company while not pressing a general engagement, Palmer turned to his staff and ordered them to pass word that the column was shifting into a line of battle and would slowly advance toward Martinsville. He knew that he most likely held the advantage, and if the Confederates resembled the description that the corporal had provided in any way, then they would surely flee or surrender instead of making a stand. As the Tenth Michigan wheeled into line of battle across the hillside, Palmer loosed his hand, and the line of over five hundred men advanced in mechanical unison. Traversing the pasture, breaking line only to avoid ill-placed obstacles, the regiment made short order of its advance and began to move through the tree line within sight of the advance guard's skirmish line.[168]

Leave Nothing for the Rebellion to Stand Upon

Halting the advance, Palmer rode close enough to dismount within observation range of Martinsville. After a brief conversation with the captain of the advance guard, who only reiterated the scene that the corporal had painted for Palmer, the commander of the First Brigade crept down to the advance outpost and drew his glasses from his belt. Surveying what he could see of the body of soldiers, it was evident that his opponents held no real semblance of central authority. While clearly a military encampment, most of the Rebels were scattered amongst the front lawns and shaded alleys of the town.

Palmer was satisfied that he was face to face with an unruly foraging party from one of the western armies occupying central North Carolina. "Dear God," he thought, "they certainly are a long way from their central command." Pondering intently as his body jostled along with the gallop of his mount, he thought, "I wonder what brought them all the way into this corner of Virginia." Abating his curiosity, he dismissed his thoughts. "No matter, they are here and I am going to deal with them."[169]

Having decided to engage the mystery Confederate force, which incidentally belonged to James Wheeler, brother of the Confederate cavalryman who had embarrassed the raid's namesake the previous year, Palmer ordered the advanced skirmishers to keep their intervals while withdrawing their outpost to their main company's line. Palmer instructed the commander of his skirmishers to leave enough space between intervals as to allow the remainder of the regiment ample room to pass without causing significant shifts in their line of battle. Afterward, the helmsman of the advance guard would consolidate his company and follow the charge in reserve, deploying his men at his discretion or at Palmer's command.

Reflecting as his mount softly trotted to his regimental line, the Quaker warrior informed the various company commanders of their role and objective in clearing the town. Following the establishment of contingent rendezvous and rallying points, Palmer issued the silent order to advance. Pushing through the thick underbrush, in which the skirmish line had found defilade, the jittery commander gave the order for charge to be sounded as the advancing line began to break clear of the thickets and emerged onto the open ground surrounding Martinsville.

The shrill ring of the bugle call was all the sensation needed to thrust the command forward in a great lunge, which exuded a force that could easily have been confused with the onset of a spring thundershower. The unsuspecting, lackluster Confederates, who were busying themselves with the preparation of the ensuing day's marching rations over impromptu cook fires, were roused from their leisurely afternoon's work by the unsuspected bugle call. Without prompt from their superiors, company-level officers ordered their men to arms and into the saddle, abandoning the auxiliary equipment that had been foolishly strewn around the makeshift campsites.

The few Confederates who had kept their carbines nearby brought them to the ready while attempting to hurriedly pack their strewn belongings and grab for the reins of their mounts. After the saddles began to fill, an intermittent volley was thrown at the charging Federal troopers, having no effect on their rate of closure. Withdrawing to the main thoroughfare, the Confederates formed their battle line just in time to exchange fire with the dismounting soldiers of Palmer's command.

The fight was wholly one-sided, as the ill-prepared Confederates were engulfed with repeating arms fire. As the flanking companies of the Tenth Michigan rode down the side streets and alleys at full speed, the Confederate commander ordered his men to fall back to the eastern edge of town to avoid encirclement. Unfortunately for a handful of the Confederate troopers, the order came too late, as several were either cut down by the dismounted marksmen or surrounded as they tried to flee down the wrong avenue.[170]

At the eastern edge of town, the Confederate force dismounted a company of troopers and fired from prone or concealed positions. This staggered the advance of the mounted elements of Palmer's command, but very soon they were employing other avenues to continue their envelopment of the faltering Rebel command. Sensing that his defense of the town was a lost cause, the Rebel cavalry commander ordered his men to withdraw beyond the borders of the town to a pasture on its eastern edge. It was there that he had made note of a meandering stone wall the previous evening, when the regiment rode into Martinsville.

As the lackluster riders broke into a confusing retreat toward their masonry savior, Palmer's men surged toward the eastern edge of town. Leaving one company to clear the town of separated Confederates who may have taken to hiding in the secluded corners of the community—all the while wrangling the multitude of prisoners that had been accumulated—Palmer re-formed his line and began to pursue the Rebels. Trudging forward at a frantic pace, it was the general's hope that if the scare was kept up, he could rob his adversary of enough time to prepare an ambush or counterattack.[171]

As Wheeler's men made their way down the slope that led to the stone wall, they were surely unaware of the natural disadvantage that the position afforded them. The wall in question was located at the base of a hill, and in the grips of panic, the officer had led his men to an obstacle that afforded no protection whatsoever and only served to exacerbate their dangerous situation. Haphazardly, Confederate troopers dismounted and filed into a battle line behind the wall moments before Palmer's men crested the top of the hill. Casting his eyes down at the events unfolding, Palmer could not believe his luck as he mused, "This must be the dumbest son-of-a-bitch in the entire rebellion." Ordering his men to halt their advance, he shook out two companies to dismount and form a prone firing line at the crest of the hill.[172]

By this point, the entrenched troopers were firing into Palmer's men with a startling accuracy that was most unexpected considering their lost nerve. As Palmer began to accumulate wounded men, he ordered the detached companies to open fire. The effects were instantaneous and devastating.

It was at this point that the one obstruction every military strategist knew to be of instantaneous benefit to a defending army became a mass grave for its employers. As the men of the Tenth Michigan fired down onto the Confederates with their Spencer repeating rifles, it became gravely apparent to the butternut-clad men that their chosen line of resistance was not the blessing it had first appeared. After enduring a few minutes of selective fire from the Federal troopers, who had a clear vantage point of the entire Confederate line beyond the wall, the officer in charge of the men braving the hellish fury ordered a retreat. As the men scrambled down the pasture toward their mounts, they were exposed to more rapid fire, which exacted deadly results.[173]

Following the Confederate flight from Martinsville, Palmer's survey of the butcher bill proved what he had suspected: the engagement had been extremely one-sided. The force that Palmer engaged on the afternoon of the seventh ranged in size from 250 to 500 men. Of those, approximately two dozen were killed or wounded in the rolling fight that spanned Martinsville and its eastern outskirts. More telling of the expediency of the attack was that 20 men and their mounts were captured inside Martinsville. The tradeoff was by no means bloodless. For all of the pain and suffering extracted from the Confederates, Palmer was forced to bear the cost of 1 officer killed and 5 men wounded at various points throughout the engagement.[174]

The engagement at Martinsville was the first warning the Confederate government had of Stoneman's intention to move his command back into North Carolina. Unlike his movement out of the Grand Old State a few days earlier, his reentry came as a wide swath across the landscape and not a massive single column progressing through a gap. While the First Brigade followed the road through Kennedy Gap, bound for Martinsville—and beyond that, North Carolina—the remainder of the command advanced toward North Carolina by way of Patrick County, Virginia. Following the engagement with James Wheeler's men, the venture into North Carolina was relatively uneventful, with only horses, fodder and food being relieved from the hands of the populace.[175]

As the Second and Third Brigades that accompanied Stoneman moved through the border county, local lore tells of an unfortunate betrayal of a local notable at the hands of his neighbors. According to accounts recorded by later generations, a local man of means by the surname Staples knew that the raiders were progressing toward his home and that the estate would almost certainly be reduced by the marauders in search of the notable fortune that resided within. Less prophetic than common sense, the assumption proved correct, as the troopers had yet to conduct any major looting of a Southern estate, and their ravenous appetite was in need of abatement. Searching his mind, Staples recalled a poor white man in the area who would almost certainly not be subject to molestation. After bundling up his silverware and other trinkets of value, the proprietor negotiated safe harbor for his treasure in exchange for a price.[176]

With few erroneous details outstanding, the Virginian patriarch correctly surmised his doom, as the property was rapidly searched. Although a few minor articles were relieved from his possession, nothing of consequential value was found by the raiders. However, Staples had been foolish enough to encourage his neighbors to engage in his scheme. Naturally, when other estates were pressed by the greedy fingers of the raiders, Staples's plan became the sacrificial lamb offered in an effort to save their holdings. Upon hearing the reiteration of a massive horde of valuables under the care of a local dirt farmer, the troopers decided to investigate.[177]

After arriving on the property and interrogating the farmer for a few moments, the coveted trove was handed over without the need for violence. Learning the fate of his silver, Staples assumed that it was lost to the fortunes of war. However, a few hours later, a rider from Stoneman's staff arrived at his doorstep. It appears that the general was adamant in his stance that no civilian property would be taken, and after the existence of the purloined silver was brought to his attention, he ordered it to be returned to its rightful owners—a scene that was surely repeated countless times during the raid's progression through North Carolina and Virginia.[178]

Following the progression of the Second and Third Brigades into North Carolina, the command encamped at Danbury on the afternoon of April 9 in an attempt to allow enough time for the division to reunite and rest. On the morning of the tenth, the First Brigade arrived and brought with it an unfortunately expected sight: camp followers. As the three brigades moved

The conundrum created by the large-scale emancipation of blacks in occupied territories was one that was never truly solved by the end of the war. In this period illustration, Stoneman holds a conversation with representatives of the camp followers who had begun to slow his progress. *Courtesy of Douglas W. Bostick.*

across a wide expanse of land, they had accumulated desperate renegade slaves, who had sought to gain their freedom by following the troopers as closely as their legs would allow. Well aware of the problems that would be presented by trying to move a large body of noncombatants alongside a small body of men, whose very survival depended on expedience behind enemy lines, Stoneman decided to send the followers back to Knoxville.[179]

Assigning a small detachment from the Second Brigade with the honors, the fugitive slaves were escorted west under guard. Upon their arrival in Knoxville, the men of military age were pressed into service in the 119th United States Colored Troops, which fell under the auspices of Colonel William Bartlett. Following their induction into military service, the new inductees were then transferred to Camp Nelson, Kentucky, for their muster. However, by the completion of their muster on May 16, the regiment was too late for the ball, having yet to complete basic training by the cessation of hostilities. After a year of precarious peacetime duty under hellacious circumstances, the regiment disbanded in April 1866.[180]

Of the men who followed Stoneman's escort into Tennessee, most of the names are lost to history. However, a cross section of the few known individuals paints a picture of privation and physical hardship, even in the midst of peacetime service. Six emancipated men from Patrick County, Virginia—Jack Reynolds, George Gray, Peter Gray, Samuel Tatum, Edmund Hylton and Jacob Reynolds—all joined at the bequest of Bartlett. However, a closer examination of their service records unveils death and disability due to preventable infirmities wrought by common ailments. While Jacob and George died in a camp outbreak of measles, the survivors hardly fared better. The remainder of the Patrick County men received a pension due to rheumatism and measles, infirmities brought about by what was termed "exposure."[181]

By the morning of the tenth, inclement weather had returned, perpetually fluctuating between a steady stream and a misty gust of rain. While desperately deserving a reprieve from further advancement, Stoneman could not afford to let the newly arrived First Brigade rest at the expense of slowing the Second and Third Brigades. Knowing that the First Brigade needed the closest assignment possible to that of a respite, the general detached Palmer and his men again on a paced foray to Salem, North Carolina. It was Stoneman's intention that a leisurely advance would afford the mounts of the First Brigade time to take ample fodder. Upon their arrival in Salem, the First Brigade was to destroy a clothing factory known to be in the town and ruin railroad bridges in the vicinity. Following the completion of its assignment, the brigade was to reunite with the remainder of the division in the neighborhood of Salisbury.[182]

Enshrouded in a constant cold drizzle and mist, Palmer moved his men along the road leading to Salem. Home guardsmen were conspicuously absent along the route as the brigade passed local farms without incident. It was not until Palmer's advance guard, a squad of twelve men selected from the Fifteenth Pennsylvania, approached the surrounding pastureland of Salem that the home guard made its presence known. About midafternoon, as the spires of the town began to crown the distant horizon, the fragment noticed five or six pickets intermittently scattered about the opposing edge of the field. The leader of the squad, a corporal by the surname of Cozens, ordered his men to maneuver out of column and into line of battle. Observing that the Union scouts intended to advance, the handful of home guardsmen willfully obliged the unspoken intent of the troopers and retreated in the direction of Salem.[183]

However, as the fair-weather soldiers withdrew from their post, one stalwart Confederate stood his ground and loosed a poorly aimed shot in the direction of the advancing line. With the piercing scream of a spinning projectile filling the air, the raiders could not believe their eyes or ears—this man was truly demonstrating a level of audacity that bordered on insanity. It was at that point that the troopers' eyes deceived them further. As they swiftly galloped across the neglected hay crop, the solitary amateur soldier stood in the middle of the pastureland without the benefit of defilade and rammed another cartridge home. As the other home guardsmen clicked spurs to mounts and sped off toward Salem, the wayward champion of the sleepy hamlet fired another hermit's volley in the direction of the advancing troopers.[184]

Following the redundantly unnerving sensation of a second musket ball lofted in their direction, the troopers surged forward at the bequest of Smith Cozens. As the troopers bore down on him from across the field, the insanity-gripped home guardsman swiftly reloaded and fired yet another round at the ever-nearing troopers, thus completing his demonstration as a Southern marksman by firing three shots to no avail. Understanding that to remain any longer at his post was to risk an almost certain untimely demise, the Confederate mounted his horse and rode off to rejoin his already flighty comrades at a full gallop.[185]

The pursuit was on. The affronted troopers, irately emboldened by the audacity of the lone combatant, pressed hard to close the gap. As one rider remembered, "Their blood was up," and tunnel vision blinded them to an even more peculiar sight amassing in front of them. About the time that the troopers rounded the bend into Salem, a gathering of thirty or so men walked directly into their path with arms and hats waving in a vain effort to flag down the predators closing in on their prey.[186]

Riding on with little heed paid to the assembly of men gathered at the limits of the town, the troopers rode directly to the town post office. There, they burst in and commandeered the parcels that resided within. It was at this point that the heroic advance guards' fortunes turned. Having been dispatched at a considerable distance, but remaining within earshot of the main body, Palmer had personally directed Corporal Cozens to halt within sight of Salem so as not arouse an unneeded alarm from the populace. Having exited the post office expecting to be met with accolades, they were instead chastised directly by Palmer, who was fresh from a conversation with the mass of arms and hats that the charging troopers had so conveniently ignored.[187]

The enthusiastic mob was yet another manifestation of the ever-evolving, late-war Confederate tradition of the conciliatory welcoming committee, albeit a larger one than that to which the command had been accustomed. Under the leadership of the mayor of Salem, Joshua Boner, and the mayor of nearby Winston, Thomas J. Wilson, local notables ranging from the headmaster of the local female academy to the local clerk of court had met in Salem with the intention of circumventing the advancing troopers on the outskirts of town in order to declare the town an open city. While the advance guard was in no temperament to hear the desperate pleas of local notables who wished to see their community spared the torch, Palmer and his staff were much more accommodating.[188]

The welcoming commission, fearing the worst from their visitors, attempted to knuckle under in grand fashion. In a sign of timid hospitality, Palmer and his staff were offered the mayor's home as headquarters. Continuing this vein of rapidly inspired patriotism, the residents of the female academy unfurled the American flag from a second-story window, much to the delight of the passing troopers. While the majority of the town tried to present the illusion of loyalty to the old flag, the clerk of court, John Blackburn, busied himself with hiding all the Confederate dockets and court papers at various residences throughout town as he pantomimed social calls to his neighbors.[189]

Continuing their subversive resistance to the raiders, the valuable cache of cotton cloth that the brigade was out to destroy was quietly transferred to the confines of private residences for concealment and safekeeping a bundle at a time. At the female academy, which happily cheered on the raiders with one side of its forked tongue, a concealment scheme of grand scale was inaugurated. In the cellar of the headmaster's house, bricks were removed from a wall, and a cavity was created with the purpose of masking the school's valuables. This nook was employed for the few remaining weeks

One of the many buildings that compose the campus of the Salem Female College and Academy, which avoided molestation thanks in part to the cunning of the school faculty and the charm of the student body. *Courtesy of the Library of Congress.*

The basement under the main hall of the school was utilized to hide many of the valuables belonging to the institution and its inhabitants. *Courtesy of the Library of Congress.*

of the war. Across the yard at the schoolhouse proper, the headmaster went so far as to hide his two prized black horses in a storage room beneath the main hall of the academy.[190]

Perhaps aiding the swift development of the raiders' newfound naivety was the presence of the Moravian monastery in town. Intermixed amongst the welcoming commission that attempted to greet the raiders were monks of the Moravian denomination, a religious order that traces its origins back to the Reformation-era teachings of Jan Hus in Bohemia and one that held a special place in the hearts of many members of the First Brigade. Tradition holds that Palmer's heart was softened due to the fact that the presence of the Moravians reminded him of experiences with similar members of the faith during his childhood.[191]

While this traditional story may not pass the smell test at first, it is certain that officers on Palmer's staff were schoolmates with the head Moravian reverend in Salem, and his presence on the welcoming committee instantly rekindled all the affection and warmth that college classmates harbor. Luckily for the study of this occurrence of fate during the war, the monks were insightful enough to make a detailed record of Palmer's occupation of Salem in their diaries. These records paint a picture of the quintessential example of benevolence at the hand of a victor toward the vanquished. The military situation presented by the monks' records outlined a body of two thousand conquerors, whose commander took every step to ensure that neither person nor property would be harmed and that business should be conducted as usual within the town.[192]

Bethabara Moravian Church in Salem, as it stood in 1936. *Courtesy of the Library of Congress.*

That evening, Palmer's brigade encamped along the high ground of a nearby creek and feasted off the large government stores residing within Salem—a gorging that resulted in not so much as a single egg being relieved from the local populace. While a few horses were commandeered with reimbursement, Palmer's affinity toward the little borough was apparently so strong that the cotton mill he was ordered to burn in town was spared. However, while his tenure in Salem was abounding with good will and Southern hospitality, Palmer was dispatched to the area to undertake a dire task: further destruction of the railroad infrastructure. Following the establishment of his headquarters, he began to subdivide his command just for that very purpose.[193]

Once again destined to continue its arduous journey without reprieve, the Fifteenth Pennsylvania was severed from the First Brigade's camp east of Salem at approximately 9:30 p.m. on the tenth. It was accompanied by orders to cripple the rail lines east of Salem in the direction of Florence and Jamestown. For this purpose, the regiment was splintered beyond recognition. With a company-sized rear guard falling under the auspices of Lieutenant Seldon L. Wilson and a secondary battalion-sized expedition down the Kernersville Road under Captain Adam Kramer, the regiment infested the countryside. While the arrival into Salem had been relatively uneventful, save the solitary display of bravado of a wayward home guard member, the ride east of Salem was not without its moments of warm action.[194]

The first to experience the throat-clinching excitement following the pleasant reprieve in Salem was Kramer's detachment, which had ridden all night and arrived on the western outskirts of Florence about sun-up. Their arrival into town was heralded by the whistle of a departing train, which naturally garnered the attention of the raiders, who spurred their mounts in an effort to run down the unseen locomotive. Following a short but expedient ride through the town and into the hamlet of Jamestown, where the depot resided, the advance guard under Captain Franklin Remont discovered a train struggling to gain the initial inertia needed to move its own weight. The crewmen had been tipped off to the presence of the raiders, and only a fraction of the locomotive's cars had been loaded before the engineer saw fit to make good his escape. In addition to the four loaded cars of seven trailing the engine, six men were taken captive, two of whom were officers.[195]

Following their brief burst of excitement at Jamestown, the fragment under Captain Kramer set out for the Deep River with the intention of burning the large covered trestle spanning the rust-colored body. In the meantime, Kramer's advance guard under Captain Remont departed Jamestown with orders to penetrate as far east into North Carolina as possible. No sooner had the small fragment departed from the hamlet than thick fog began to envelop the countryside, forcing the troopers to advance cautiously toward the river. Their caution was well deserved, as a company-sized collection of home guard was gathering on the hills opposite the trestle.[196]

Kramer's men descended upon the trestle swiftly and without warning and discovered a two-man guard protecting the structure; both guardsmen surrendered without a fight as their comrades on the hill left the duo to their own providence. Following the capture of the trestle, the reduced battalion went to work destroying it, and within the space of thirty minutes, the entire edifice was engulfed in flames. With fog becoming ever present, Kramer decided that a splintered command was not the most advantageous disposition for his men. After dispatching riders with orders to reunify the command, Remont's fragment was stumbled upon by the remainder of the battalion at Florence on the afternoon of the eleventh.[197]

Having placed only a few miles between the Florence town limits sign and his detachment, Kramer was welcomed by the sight of Remont's company and its swiftly accumulated spoils of war. The morning efforts of the subordinate captain netted the command sixty fresh horses and mules. Along with this collection of beasts, thirty-two enlisted men and three officers were taken prisoner. After the presentation of the trove by the detachment, troopers were shaken out of the column with orders to destroy the Confederate munitions factory in town.[198]

Under the auspices of Lieutenant Ed Smith, five men inspected the factory and took inventory of it prior to incineration. The factory contained eight hundred finished weapons, as well as parts enough to complete another twenty-five hundred stands. Also contained in the factory was the machinery to mill weaponry parts and instruments for the assaying of precious metals. While it was mentioned in later recollections that there were small amounts of both gold and silver present for the purpose of conversion into Confederate bullion, no official record was made of such metals—a sure sign that the valuable elements found their way into the pockets of troopers with rather sticky fingers.[199]

Following the survey of the factory and the initiation of its destruction, men from Remont's company were ordered to ride down to the depot in Florence and burn the stores of supplies that had been unearthed there. The cache that fell victim to the torch, along with the supply depot itself, contained one thousand long arms, fifty barrels of flour, two barrels of molasses, twelve hundred pounds of salt, five bales of jean cotton cloth, an unmentionably large amount of bacon and two railroad cars full of raw cotton. Following the disbursement of the edibles amongst the troopers, the surplus was reduced to cinders.[200]

All the while, Confederate presence in the region began to grow, and Kramer's pickets were quite successful in capturing lost combatants who wandered into their lines. In a sign that many Southern combatants thought the war to be rapidly approaching its end, the beleaguered Spartans began to surrender under circumstances where they obviously possessed the upper hand. In one instance, early during the evening of the eleventh on the outskirts of Florence, Private George Alexander from Company I of the Fifteenth Pennsylvania single-handedly captured an entire courier detachment consisting of one officer and twelve mounted men. His catch was fully armed and capitulated without firing a shot. Adding to the reputation of the same company, Private Samuel Wampler captured three troopers acting as an advance guard for a rapidly approaching cavalry force without so much as placing his prominent finger on the trigger.[201]

Informed by Wampler that there was a sizeable Confederate cavalry presence in the vicinity, Kramer decided to withdraw his battalion from the area around Florence and Jamestown with the intention of rejoining the main body. His side adventure had been most profitable. The majority of his men were now riding fresh mounts, with the slightly worn but still serviceable mounts trailing behind. Fully resupplied with rations and with the munitions factory exploding behind it, the battalion struck off at a leisurely trot, leaving elements of Ferguson's Confederate Cavalry stranded on the opposite bank of the Deep River, with a flaming bridge blocking any possibility of pursuit.[202]

As the battalion returned to the main body resting at Salem, it brought with it fifty prisoners pilfered from the area surrounding Florence and Jamestown, most of whom had been identified as secessionists by their Loyalist neighbors. Observing the cavalcade of troopers into Salem, one Moravian diarist noted that the detachment mistakenly took the wrong road into town and arrived at the local Moravian Field of Souls, an organization of graveyard particular to that denomination divided by sex, station in life and church hierarchy. In a sign of the regiment's reverence for the brethren and people of Salem, the troopers dismounted and walked their mounts through the cemetery. Going so far as to remove their covers from their heads, the solemn members of the procession continued their demonstration of reverence well past the graveyard.[203]

Kramer's men were not the only riders dispatched to render the local railroads useless. One hundred men, under the guidance of Major Abraham Garner, were ordered to ride toward the northeast and burn a trestle spanning Reedy Fork Creek, a critical point on the newly constructed Confederate infrastructure commonly referred to as the Danville Railroad. Unbeknownst to the command, Danville was currently the temporary capital of the Confederate government, and successfully severing the line would guarantee that the renegade government would be cornered in Virginia without an avenue by which to reach the support of the remaining Confederate armies in the field. As with similar fragments of the First Brigade, Garner's men were instructed to progress toward their assignment at a leisurely pace to conserve their mounts' energy, a decision that proved to be a fatal mistake in the Union's efforts to corral the renegade government.[204]

Arriving along a rock-infested waterway, the operatives were greeted by the realization of the difficulty of their task. The trestle was less than two years old and constructed of dense hardwood. Therefore, the unseasoned bridge would not spark like the pinewood constructions that the soldiers had encountered previously. After over two hours of chopping away at the pilings in an effort to splinter them, the bridge was finally lit with some difficulty by midafternoon on the eleventh.[205]

While the primary concentration of the detachment labored away on the bridge, Sergeant John K. Marshall was busy with warm work. Detached to lead the rearguard, his detail was constantly bombarded by mounted Confederate skirmishers belonging to Colonel James Wheeler's command. After two hours, he had yet to lose a man but had inflicted little, if any damage, of his own. However, due to the constant arrival of Confederate reinforcements, if the detachment did not withdraw with relative haste after the trestle's destruction, Marshall reported it would be embroiled in a fight it could not win.[206]

The reason for the growing Confederate presence that afternoon was discovered slightly later in the evening. Extracted from a captured Confederate picket, word came that the entire Rebel cabinet had fled Danville bound for Greensboro and had crossed over the Reedy Fork trestle within an hour of when Garner's men had arrived at the site. The specter of Wheeler's men and the growing Confederate presence in the area were to ensure the Confederate administration's escape. When later informed of his narrow escape from Danville, the renegade president of the Confederacy, Jefferson Davis, remarked that "a miss is as good as a mile."[207]

With the First Brigade reunited in Salem, Palmer dispatched the entire Fifteenth Pennsylvania under Colonel Charles Betts in the direction of Greensboro to ascertain the situation there and make a harassing demonstration against Beauregard's growing force. Traveling through the night, the regiment received word from its advance guard that a sizeable force of Confederate cavalry was encamped along the road a few miles outside Greensboro. Consolidating his troopers, Betts charged headlong into the encampment at sun-up with the intention of scattering it and rendering the opposing cavalry useless to pursue the First Brigade when it withdrew from Salem. The pitched charge was undertaken with pistol and saber in hand—all the while, Betts ordered his men to yell as loudly as possible in order to rouse fear and confusion within the Confederate ranks.[208]

The regiment in question was the Third South Carolina Cavalry under the command of Colonel Thomas J. Johnson. With the sight of a full regiment of mounted men bearing down on them at a full gallop with sabers and pistols drawn, the South Carolinians, who were busy cooking their morning rations, either scattered to the four winds or surrendered without a fight. Among the men who resorted to the latter were Colonel Johnson and his staff. While the Third South Carolina had rarely fought as a cohesive unit, most of the men having occupied their terms of service protecting various portions of South Carolina at the company level and avoiding the large battles of the major theaters, the majority of the regiment embarrassed its less-than-stellar record that morning by surrendering in mass. Proud of his former regiment's haul, Palmer later recorded in Betts's Congressional Medal of Honor citation that the colonel's men took just as many prisoners that morning as they had brought into the engagement.[209]

Following an organization of the prisoners, the breakfast that the Confederates were cooking was enjoyed by the Federal troopers. A further inspection of the camp uncovered luxuries such as peach brandy, chicken potpie and tobacco, all of which were enjoyed by the victors while they lasted. Following the nosh, the prisoners were marched off toward Salem, while a detachment under Lieutenant Selden Wilson was sent to burn the bridge over Buffalo Creek. Although the men of the splinter were unnerved by the massive Confederate presence in the area and feared a bloody demise, their work was done in short order due to the dry Carolina pine of which the bridge was constructed.[210]

While securing the bridge, Wilson's men came across an old farmer and relieved him of his tools. In a heartbreaking example of the critical necessity of even the smallest implement to the survival of the yeoman farmer, the old man begged to not have his freshly honed axe spoiled by striking it across the trestle. Bargaining for the fate of his simple iron tool, the aging man agreed to assist the troopers in burning the bridge on the condition that they did not use his axe—because he touted that he was as good a Union man as God lets live. Following the igniting of the bridge, the troopers parted with the relieved farmer and left the area.[211]

Intent not to press their luck any further with such a large Confederate presence in the vicinity, the troopers rode hard toward their main body. Upon reunion with the main body at Salem, they were oblivious to the fact that they were less than two miles from the Confederate president's train, which was resting on a spur line on the outskirts of Greensboro. It must have been devastating for the troopers when this information reached their ears—a spoiled elation that caused their hearts to sink when they came to the realization that if they had not feared for their own necks and pressed deeper into Confederate-held territory, the raiders might have had the opportunity to cart off the Rebel leader. Later, the lament only intensified, as these very same troopers would spend the better part of the next two months trying to achieve that very task.[212]

On the afternoon of April 12, four years to the day after the conflict was inaugurated, the First Brigade departed from Salem bound for a reunion of the entire command at Salisbury. Palmer left the town in the same condition that his men had found it and did little to inconvenience the populace. However, the same can not be said for the Confederates sent to pursue them. Elements of James Wheeler's cavalry rode into the town on the sixteenth with shattered discipline and ransacked the local stores and pilfered many private residences. Looting was so extensive that a regiment of infantry who remained loyal to the command of Beauregard was dispatched to Salem and assaulted the wayward troopers, scattering the opportunists and relegating them to the status of outliers. The internal squabble that left several Confederates dead on either side was an ominous heralding of the lawlessness that would engulf the former Confederacy in the ensuing months.[213]

By this point, the Confederate cavalry commands, with the exception of those under the command of Wade Hampton in the Carolinas and Nathan

Whether exaggerated or not, the pilfering of Southern towns at the hands of wayward Confederate soldiers was a real, and sadly common, threat in the closing days of the war. *Courtesy of the Library of Congress.*

Bedford Forrest in the Gulf States, had witnessed a serious erosion of discipline and morale. From the abandonment of Virginia by the Confederate government until the latest weeks of spring, Southern civilians were equally worried about renegade Confederate bands and outliers as they were about the occupying Federal army. Unfortunately for the noncombatants of the defeated South, all three sought to prey on the helpless civilians in the confusion created by a dying conflict.[214]

While the First Brigade was venturing out of the area around Salem in a very hospitable manner, the Second and Third Brigades under the direct command of Stoneman advanced toward Salisbury with malign intent. Passing through Germantown and Bethania, both Moravian communities similar to Salem, the raiders behaved poorly in comparison to their First Brigade counterparts. On the evening of April 10, the inhabitants of Bethania, in the midst of a Holy Week service, were alerted mid-sermon that Federal cavalry had entered the town. To their surprise, upon exiting the church, the flock was welcomed by the sight of troopers ransacking their homes and stuffing their haversacks to the brim with purloined valuables. Stoneman, personally headquartered in the home of Elais Schaub, was relatively detached from his men as the finest Cossacks born of the

Cumberland Plateau picked the town clean, going so far as to commandeer every mount in the town.[215]

On the morning of the eleventh, Stoneman's column moved on to the banks of the Yadkin River and crossed at Shallow Ford, a few miles west of Winston. Assigned to guard the ford, the amateur soldiers were surprised, as they had failed to post pickets, and the entire body was quickly dispatched, leaving more than one hundred deserted muskets along the banks of the river. Following their successful re-fording of the Yadkin, a smooth undertaking in stark contrast to the debacle that occurred when the command first crossed the river, Stoneman led his men at the head of a column that was bound for Mocksville to the southwest.[216]

At the outskirts of Mocksville, the command's advance guard was greeted by sporadic fire originating from Elisha Creek. The levelers of the ineffective volleys were a patchwork collection of old men and boys who took it upon themselves to engage the rumored mountain bushwhackers who were marauding through the area, a problem that had been most troublesome for their community in the preceding years. Unfortunately for the small band of improvised home guardsmen, the men whom they drew beads upon were not advantageous bands of bushwhackers but instead the most hardened Federal elements in the entirety of Western North Carolina. Upon realizing their mistake, the men bolted for the brush as the raiders lobbed a few ineffective rounds in the direction of the tree-lined creek.[217]

The men of the forward element were most unnerved by the audacious actions of the armed civilians. Fearing that Mocksville could easily transform into a hornet's nest of partisan fire upon their entry into the town, the men began to actively petition their commander for the town's incineration. However, Stoneman was quick to overturn their request and reassured his command that their fear of a partisan trap was unfounded war nerves.[218]

Upon entering the town, the riders spread about and began to relieve the populace of their excess foodstuffs. With many troopers finding respite in isolated patches of shade along the streets, the citizens were required to cook a meal for their occupying aggressors, while the more energetic raiders ransacked their homes in search of valuables. As the men ate in shifts, others burned the cotton mill in town. Although much of the mischief was undertaken without unwonted destruction, according to local tradition, one drunken soldier lit a woman's bed on fire in her house. Whether the act was undertaken in malice or the result of an accident remains a mystery. Following their brief occupation of Mocksville, the two brigades progressed toward Salisbury and made camp a dozen or so miles away, plotting their long-awaited liberation of the notorious Confederate prison there.[219]

"The People Are Looking for Stoneman to Come Here"

an alive! They're horrible!" The thought evolved as a gasp of air
filling his nostrils created a gurgling sensation as it intermixed with
the water pouring into his slackened jaw. "Are they even trying to hit us?"
The young private began to smirk, finding amusement at the ironic timing
of this whimsical musing's arrival as he thrust his body forward toward the
north bank of Grant's Creek. Wedged beneath his left arm was one end of a
long and increasingly slippery pinewood plank that stretched for several feet
beyond the rhythmic chopping of the private's legs. All the while, his nails
burrowed steadily deeper into the end of the board in a vain attempt to keep
it from tipping horizontally into the water, thus causing the erratic swimmer
to lose control. His normally kempt, brushed and polished uniform was
reduced to rolled shirtsleeves as a preventative measure intended to relieve
the struggling swimmer of the added burden of weight, which the absorbent
wool uniform would surely bring after saturation in the swift-flowing creek.
Increasing his efforts as the north bank came within reach, the private
grabbed at the water with his free arm, frantically dividing the current as if
he were dragging his lifeless torso across dry ground.

Consumed by his intense endeavor, the private's mind became detached
from the horrific reality of his predicament. While the youth advanced in
meditative delirium, he did so oblivious to the sporadic shower of droplets
created by Confederate musket balls, which pierced the water with a velocity
that sent back-jets several feet into the air. The bubbling effect projected

from the creek as a result of the perforative missiles was augmented by yet another peculiar sight: the disintegration of the normally placid current to that of an erratic wake induced by dozens of quasi-submerged bodies floundering in a frenzied state. As the private successfully navigated past countless flying limbs protruding from bodies of enlisted men who were pursuing dry land with equal adamance, his senses bestowed upon him yet another unforeseen truth. Welcomed by the viscous sensation of creek-bank mud sieving between the fingers of his right hand as he thrust it into the ground in an effort to heave himself free of his watery impediment, the private came to the realization that not a single man had been so much as wounded in the initial crossing.

"This caps the climax of maddens." The knot that prevented the dripping private from swallowing dissipated as the unnatural revelation finally began to take hold. "Those dammed secesh aren't even trying; every cussed one of them are over shooting." As the debilitating tension left his shoulders, the plank was simultaneously ripped from the confines of his arms, ferociously pried from his clutches by an unseen corporal. The bewildering effects of the morning's work on the private were reflected in the pale complexion and hollow stare that encompassed his face as the shivering young man followed with his eyes the course of his delivery up the bank as it passed from the hands of faceless soldier to faceless soldier. Within a matter of seconds, the compulsion to complete his assignment rose up from within, forcing him to turn once again toward the creek. Lunging down the slippery bank and toward the water, the muck-covered laborer shoved his equally miserable ascending comrades aside, desiring nothing more than to submerge his feet once more in the cold, gritty water of the creek.

Wading through the frigid, swiftly moving water to an appropriate depth, the nameless combatant bent his quivering knees and thrust forward into the depths of the creek. His spirit seemed impervious to the sheer terror-infused panic that gripped the other men of the company as they scampered from the friendlier confines of the Union-held north bank to the heavily defended south bank. All of this madness was the result of a decision by their superior officer to demonstrate his bravado as a field commander by dictating that his men retrieve the planks that the malicious Confederate defenders had wisely removed from the floor of the middle span of Grant's Creek Bridge and piled high in front of their rifle pits.[220]

"Their hearts are not in this. These men aren't even fighting." Basking in the comforting warmth that was taking hold of his body, the swimmer lapsed into deeper thought. "They are firing for show." The shaky aesthetic that the private had woven in his mind was all at once ripped in two by the hollow thud of a ball tearing through the body cavity of a returning swimmer. Right before the private's blood-splattered eyes, this unknown member of his company emitted a memory-haunting gurgle as the forceful impact of the Confederate missile submerged his head. The shock of witnessing the fragmentation of a man seized him like the grips of a vise, instilling instantaneous paralysis. The young man may have sat idly, bobbing in the water, concentrating on the gruesome scene before his eyes were it not for a fellow swimmer who struck his back in an effort to move the frozen man out of the way. The flood of returning senses washed his muddled state downstream with the flow of the current, leavening the disheartened soldier to continue his course, knowing full well that any of his previous suspicions as to the intentions of his adversaries were faulty and that he was indeed in true danger.

Clutching fists full of mud augmented with a thatchwork of roots and canebrake, the trooper scaled the increasingly steep and muddy bank with demoniacal persistence. The initial gentle rise of the bank had been worn to a vertical cliff after being subjected to erosion by the repetitive ascent of a dismounted company crawling up it. In a desperate attempt at final refuge, the troopers clambered up the bank in the prone position as they prepared to make an attempt at the ever-dwindling pile of pinewood planks stacked in front of the Confederate defenses. Cresting the summit of the bank, the saturated air fluttered with flying projectiles, whispering a reminder that his last moments could be upon him. Crouching as he scurried toward the pile, the young soldier's eyes were locked on the plank he thought could be extracted with relative expediency and not result in hesitation, which would expose him further to the barrage from the Confederate position. With the Rebel balls singing their morbid, spine-curling ballad as they tore through the air, the private's mind narrowed into a surreal dream, where the only two inhabitants of this world were his hunkered form and the chosen plank.

Drenched in fear and locked in tunnel vision, the next few moments were lost to the young man's memory. Upon retuning to his senses, the private was greeted by the piercing howls of a sergeant, who had grabbed hold of his shirt and was pulling him up the northern bank. In this befuddled state, the private came to the understanding that he was not to hand the plank to the bucket brigade as he had upon the completion of his first trip across the creek. Instead, he was to ascend the bank and personally hand the plank over to the unfortunate souls who had been designated as carpenters. Summiting the bank while dragging the heavy plank behind him, the weight of which was later alleviated when an unseen compatriot grabbed the entrenched end, the private ran with his head so close to the Carolina clay that its musk filled his nostrils as he neared the wooden skeleton that had previously served as a bridge.

The men who brought the planks to the bridge were scattered intermittently along both sides of the dirt road in order to construct an avenue to pass the planks forward from soldier to soldier while staying as close to prone as possible to avoid Confederate fire. At the head of these twin columns of human bodies, both of which consisted of men who were making deep imprints in the muck with their buttons in an attempt to melt into the muddy road, were the unfortunate souls selected to serve as carpenters. The regimental marksmen formed a line that would have ultimately dissected these snakes had it not been for the necessity of keeping the road free from obstruction in an effort to provide cover fire for the men as they worked. The only response to their harassing fire was an intermittently ineffective barrage from the surprisingly large number of cannons that dotted the south bank—a clear sign that all was not well with the Confederate fighting spirit.[221]

Captivated by the expediency of the carpenters' work, the private's nerves were calmed by their diligent demonstration of steadiness under fire. As the forward workers slew crabwise across the planks, quickly replacing one after another, the line advanced on its stomach with a speed that one would normally accomplish at a leisurely stroll. While the carpenters in the rear of the detail screamed incoherent curses of expedience toward the members of the bucket brigade who were passing the last of the planks forward, the unfortunate souls at the very front of this unusual Union advance were in dire straits. Showered with splinters of wood that were the result of Confederate balls chomping away at the wood beams that supported the structure, the unfortunate laborers neared the last few feet of their task. Although the majority of men were streaming blood from the minor lacerations that encompassed their bodies from exploding spurs of lead and flying splinters, none was directly pierced by the volleys from the Confederate infantrymen showering down on them from the south side of the bridge.

As the last plank migrated amongst the various hands that propelled it forward, the work details drawn from the Eighth and Thirteenth Tennessee began to trickle back out of musket range and clear to the sides of the road. Then, too, the carpenters began to make a hurried, crouching withdrawal to the rear as the last plank was finally wedged into place. It was at that moment that those planning the grand assault understood that their ambitions could at last materialize. Scurrying back to the line of dropped equipment left where the details had been formed a half hour earlier, the ground underneath the private's feet began to tremble. Looking up as he rearranged his accoutrements into functional order, the private witnessed the remainder of the Third Brigade storming down the Mocksville Road at a full charge. The assault was spectacular, full of the nervous energy that drives maniacs but augmented with enough discipline to maintain single-file formation in an effort to prevent a bottle neck on the narrow wooden bridge. It was widely understood by all the combatants involved that if even a solitary plank happened to jump from its loosely lodged position, then the whole charge would be bogged down, and the mounted men would become sitting ducks.[222]

As the troopers charged across the bridge, the reverberation of their mounts' hooves on the wooden planks caused the slats to bounce and snap, but not a single one was dislodged from its unsecured state. It was at that moment that the Confederates occupying the hillside were ordered to concentrate their fire on the advancing column of mounted men. However, the majority of men clad in gray uniforms undertook an action of such peculiarity that it has been remembered for generations since. While many of the men obliged their commander's order to concentrate their fire on the advancing column by drawing a deadly and precise bead on the advancing troopers, the overwhelmingly vast majority purposely fired over the heads of the advancing troopers and then defiantly refused to reload their muskets.[223]

In addition to this flagrant demonstration of treason, the well-positioned artillerymen had the audacity to fire their pieces at such an elevation that the projectiles not only soared over the heads of the charging troopers but also sailed far beyond the dismounted men providing covering fire. As the screaming troopers began to ride up the inclining road, their company commanders drew their men into line of battle and, as the bugle sounded, charged the hill headlong, expecting full well that the Confederate infantrymen were readying themselves to meet their opponents with a devastating volley of musket fire. Instead of riding abreast into the hellish muzzle flashes that had become the customary response to an assault against a fortified position, the riders were greeted by cheers for the old flag—a situation that baffled the blue-clad riders as they rode past the scores of petrified, smiling men, who were either holding their arms up in the air or waving their hats in fervent support of the charging troopers.[224]

On the Confederate side of the entrenchments, the true butternut combatants, effectively drawing beads on the troopers and inflicting mild damage, were even more taken aback by the spectacle than the Federal soldiers. Not believing their eyes, the scattered companies that were actually presenting armed resistance to the assault began to waver and then broke into a mad, panicked dash for the city of Salisbury, the strength of their awe-inspiring position having been betrayed by the very men who tended it just a few yards down the entrenchments. Their flight left the ground behind the entrenchments strewn with muskets and accoutrements. More importantly, the men who were in charge of the irreplaceable field pieces were forced to abandon them where they rested. The victory had been total, relatively bloodless and unprecedented by the events of the previous four years.[225]

The incident that occurred on April 12, 1865, known locally within Rowan County, North Carolina, as the Battle of Grant's Creek, was a microcosm of what the military prowess of the Confederacy—and even more so, the Southern psyche—had been reduced to in the closing weeks of the war. Four years out from the start of the conflict, the Confederate army found itself at the end of its rope. The assault that the Third Brigade led against the defenders of Salisbury was directed against a body of infantrymen who were largely disenchanted with the Confederate cause, under trained, infirm or press-ganged into service. As with most matters surrounding the closing weeks of the war, the defense of the vital supply depot and former prison of Salisbury was steeped in confusion. The foggy shroud of consternation created by the panic-induced scramble for refuge by the dwindling Confederate hierarchy and the defense of the last vestiges of its control castrated any attempts at keeping the city out of Union hands.

The perfect storm of bedlam created by the consolidation of the remnants of the various Confederate armies inhabiting western and central North Carolina bred an atmosphere of resentment and ill purpose. The catalyst of this problem were the many disenchanted officers who were struggling with their lateral demotions, loosely defined objectives and revolving changes in command as the last vestiges of defenders were reorganized and paper commands ceased to exist. Case in point was the lateral demotion of Pierre Gustave Toutant Beauregard from commander of all Confederate troops in the Military Division of the West, a position that granted him administrative command over all remaining soldiers in Alabama, Georgia, eastern Louisiana, Mississippi, South Carolina and Tennessee, to that of second in command of the Army of Tennessee under Joseph E. Johnston. The orders, which stripped Beauregard of the lofty lip service of theater commander, were signed as the Army of Tennessee gathered near Smithfield in preparation for its fatal encounter with Sherman's army at Bentonville and consolidated all the remaining commands in the region under Johnston's control as he made his exodus toward the Virginia border. The result of this order was Beauregard being left with effective control over a solitary corps consisting of the remaining Confederate elements in the western portion of

Seemingly everywhere during the war, Pierre Gustave Toutant Beauregard was saddled with many burdens during the late hours of the conflict that bordered on impossibilities, especially that of securing western North Carolina for the dying Confederacy. *Courtesy of the Library of Congress.*

North Carolina, while the remainder of his prescribed command under the auspices of Johnston was locked in mortal competition with the advancing Union behemoth nearly two hundred miles away.[226]

No sooner had Beauregard been dealt the blow of a lateral demotion then the old paladin was ordered by the War Department to make for western Virginia in hopes of blocking a theoretical advancement by George H. Thomas into Confederate-controlled southwestern Virginia. Knowing full well that this position would destroy any remnants of his remaining relevance, the appointment was refused outright, and Beauregard elected to remain under the auspices of Johnston. Following this self-imposed relegation, Davis ordered Beauregard to form a second independent command in the Carolinas. The decision granted Beauregard total authority over the remaining men in the vicinity of Western North Carolina and East Tennessee, an act that essentially returned him his previous area of command, albeit reduced by three quarters.[227]

As an unavoidable side effect to this late-hour reshuffle, which uprooted many longstanding chains of command, Beauregard was forced to quickly develop some trace elements of amity with estranged commands that were intermittently scattered throughout the borderlands of South Carolina and Tennessee. This epic feat was accomplished in short order by a marathon trek via rail that covered a plethora of stops between Charlotte and Greensboro, in which the general personally dictated his orders and expectations to his new subordinates. Soon after Beauregard's appointment, cavalry and infantry brigades under Winfield Scott Featherstone arrived at Salisbury en route to Greensboro, thus falling under the auspices of the debonair tactician's command. Not wasting a single moment of this windfall that was bestowed to him, the fresh arrivals were ordered to begin the construction of entrenchments along the Yadkin River northeast of the city to serve as a rallying point for the retreating Confederate government should their rout reach the western expanses of the North Carolina piedmont. Following the commencement of the western soldier's labors, conflicting orders arrived from Johnston's Army of Tennessee, and the three brigades were ordered to advance toward the northeast to secure Danville and consolidate with Johnston's army as it limped away from Bentonville.[228]

As the late-hour restructuring of the Confederate house of cards began to unfold, the inhibiting side effect that the mass consolidation had on the waning defenses of the last major depot became all too apparent. The man initially charged with the defense of the vital city, General Bradley Johnson, who had organized a force of approximately brigade strength, fell victim to this rearrangement. With word that Stoneman was advancing on either Danville or Greensboro, two cities that now, incidentally, found themselves the center of the Confederate universe, Johnston dispatched the small command via rail to defend the municipalities. No sooner had the command arrived along the Yadkin River than the intentions of Stoneman became obvious, and an infuriated Beauregard demanded the return of the large component of his command that had been pilfered by an overbearing superior officer. Although Beauregard's concerns were validated and the brigade was ordered to reverse its course, its return was impeded by the destruction inflicted at the hands of Stoneman's First Brigade on the local rail infrastructure. The end result of this misadventure was that the largest concentration of infantry in Western North Carolina would be conspicuously absent from the defense of one of the last major Confederate supply depots.[229]

The defenses that snaked along Grant's Creek were manned by what little strength Beauregard could muster from the vicinity of Salisbury. After arriving in Greensboro to hold council with the transitive president on the evening of the eleventh, the general ignored a directive from Jefferson Davis that ordered him to move his entire command to Danville in an effort to continue the same wild goose chase for Stoneman that Johnson had inaugurated. After receiving word that the mail was intercepted by raiders near a Yadkin crossing known as Shallow Ford that morning, the old Cajun stayed put and elected to defend his seat of command. Unfortunately for the fate of the vital rail town, the general's will to stand his ground far outpaced his practical ability to defend the city. Absent from Salisbury due to a request to attend an ill-timed conference with the president, the motley crew of three thousand that composed Brigadier General William M. Gardner's Brigade attempted to undertake the stand that Beauregard had initiated via proxy. Beauregard's only available force for the action was led onto the field of battle that morning by the disgraced former lieutenant general John C. Pemberton, who now held rank in the North Carolina state troops as colonel.[230]

Unfortunately for the aging colonel, his defense of Salisbury would not equal his lionhearted defense of the Gibraltar of the Mississippi, which had resulted in his surrender of a large Confederate army to Grant two Fourth of Julys previous. The men whom Pemberton had before him were a cross section of the last Confederate forces in the field. While a large minority of his men were those who were absent from the Army of Northern Virginia at the time of its surrender, either by permission or desertion, the vast majority were North Carolina home guardsmen and militia, quickly mustered to defend the valuable city. To augment this typical gathering of late-war defenders was an anomaly that had increased in presence throughout the region—a group of turncoat opportunists known as the "Galvanized Irish."[231]

These unique cadres of combatants, born of the Emerald Isle, were recruited upon arrival at various ports of entry during the early years of the conflict. After serving in the Union army for wages, having very little interest in the philosophical cause of the conflict, they surrendered at the first opportunity, either expecting to be paroled in short order or, at the very worst, given a leisurely stay in confinement. However, as the nature of the prisoner of war exchange deteriorated following the Confederate government's refusal to honor black soldiers with the status of combatants instead of labeling them insurrectionists, these Irish soldiers found themselves in the same horrific prison camp conditions as those to which their North American–born brethren were subjected. Looking for any opportunity to alleviate themselves from their situation, the Galvanized Irish were especially susceptible to offers from the Confederate hierarchy to fill much-needed enlisted vacancies in exchange for freedom from imprisonment. However, the natural side effect was that these men were just about as loyal to the Confederate cause as they were to the Union war effort.[232]

Following the reconstruction of the two middle spans of the Grant's Creek Bridge and the charge against the Confederate works by the Third and, later, Second Brigades, these Galvanized Irish were quick to turn coat for a second time and assist in the Confederate rout by refusing to fire on the charging Union soldiers. Witnessing the collapse initiated by their actions at various points along the line, the Southern-born Confederate infantrymen broke due to this irreconcilable breach. In addition to the rupture of their primary defenses initiated by the faltering Galvanized Irish, Stoneman's command was successful at severing the Confederate lines of retreat by crossing a reinforced company's strength at two fords that flanked the primary engagement.[233]

Hearing the sharp shrill of steam whistles on the battleground, the Eleventh Kentucky supplied one hundred men to cross the creek at the nearest ford above the bridge for the purpose of interrupting the railroad line that was heading out of Salisbury. Likewise, a detachment of equal strength under Lieutenant Colonel B.P. Stacy of the Thirteenth Tennessee was to cross at the nearest opportunity downstream, hook behind the defenders and draw a line of battle between them and the city. In addition to these successful undertakings, a battalion of Kentucky cavalry from an unnamed regiment was sent along the Old Salisbury Road to attempt a feint toward the city from an undefended vantage point, thus adding to the confusion and anxiety of the Confederate defenders.[234]

The bravery displayed by the men of the Third Brigade netted fruits unlike any that Stoneman had reaped during his entire career; indeed, the skirmish along Grant's Creek and the capture of Salisbury were to be Stoneman's swan song. The end result of the morning's efforts were the deprival of fourteen irreplaceable artillery sets, the capitulation of 53 officers and the surrender of 1,311 enlisted men. Furthermore, the city of Salisbury lay open before the raiders without a single organization defending it, leaving only a few scant defenders who would attempt an informal contest for the valuable real estate. As the Second and Third Brigades charged the two-mile stretch of road into Salisbury, continuing to round up countless defeated Rebels along every inch of the roadway, division provost marshal Major Sterling Hambright and chief of staff Major George F. Barnes from the Second Brigade were left with a handful of men to organize the prisoners. Later, the same men would be utilized to take account of what supplies were captured within the massive Confederate stores at Salisbury.[235]

As the troopers advanced to the city limits, Stoneman dispatched the Third Brigade to render the eastern-bound rail line useless should Beauregard attempt to muster reinforcements from Greensboro, while the Second Brigade had the honor of liberating the city of Salisbury from the hands of the Confederates. The residents of Salisbury were surprised at the speed with which the defense of the city evaporated and the raiders penetrated the interior of Salisbury. One inhabitant remembered that the raiders appeared within the town in an instant, coming from every direction and seemingly out of nowhere. Another recalled that the Yankees rode into town with swords in hand and oaths in mouth, demanding the direct obedience of the citizens in town. The same citizen, E.H.M. Summerell, later called into question the efforts to defend Salisbury. He scoffed that the Battle of Grant's Creek was by no means even a fight, as the men melted away from duty or were scattered around the line to such an extent that no more than 150 defenders could be found at any point along the line. This recollection, if credible, paints a divergent military situation that by no means echoes the grand spectacle of the 3,000 defenders later records indicated.[236]

No matter what events truly transpired at Salisbury, the citizens were deeply affected by the day's transactions, as generations of folk traditions were passed down about the raiders' entrance into the city. The wife of E.M. Ramsey recalled the horrific experience she had on the morning the troopers stormed into the town. As the various routed defenders retreated for a desperate chance at anonymity, achieved by blending into the civilian population, one Galvanized Irishman elected to make a solitary stand against the advancing troopers. The unnamed Celt, pierced through the lungs and gulping blood with every breath, staggered down the gutters of a side thoroughfare, taking the opportunity to conceal himself behind the corners of houses along his path, reloading and firing as he made his retreat through the town. Having inflicted some minor inconvenience on the troopers, they attempted to swarm him but quickly rethought their initial assault, as he proved to be an exceptional marksman, infirmities notwithstanding. Showering his position with repeating rifle fire, the Irishman abandoned it and tried to make his escape through the front yard of the Ramsey house.[237]

Attempting to reload in the deadly open air of the yard on weak legs, the young man staggered onto the piazza of the house, where he finally succumbed to his injuries and collapsed in the doorway. Braving a shower of flying lead, which inflicted considerable damage to the front of the house, Mrs. Ramsey opened the door, took hold of the Irishman and dragged his frail body inside. It was in a room on the first floor of the house that she dressed his wounds and stemmed the flow of blood that seeped from his chest. After stabilizing her patient, she had him moved to the hospital under cover of darkness.[238]

Being informed that his wounds were fatal, she returned to her home distraught that all her efforts and the attention drawn to her house were in vain. Much to her disbelief, a few weeks later she was alerted by a rap at the same door that her display of feminine bravado had launched her headlong into the annals of war. Her eyes were delighted by the sight of the Irishman, fully recovered, who had returned to give her thanks for saving him that fateful morning.[239]

It was not only the upper-class that was affected by the raiders' descent on Salisbury. Later accounts of the incident make mention of twin slaves who had lived their entire lives in the company of each other's presence. The twelve-year-old siblings, Albert and Victoria, belonged to a local family by the name of Bradshaw. The pair had been absent all morning during the initial shock of the troopers' arrival, dispatched with the family's wagon on some undocumented task. Later in the afternoon, after the raiders had settled into camp and the rabble-rousing had subsided, Victoria returned with tears streaming down her face, bearing word that her brother had unhitched the lead mule from the Bradshaws' wagon and rode off to join the raiders. Whatever became of Albert remained a mystery to his sibling, as Victoria never heard from him again.[240]

Following the securing of the city, the victorious troopers began to venture out to the local domiciles and commence the looting that was to be expected following the liberation of a Confederate-controlled venue. At the home of a local politician by the name of Archibald Henderson, who was taken to bed with a debilitating illness when Stoneman's command arrived, the raiders were deterred from entering the home by an unlikely obstacle. Mrs. Henderson had met the approaching marauders headlong with a loaded pistol clutched in a white-knuckle grip as she threatened to dispatch the first soldier who darkened the door. Naturally, the raiders withdrew, only to establish a bivouac on a nearby green space. Knowing that the scorned men would likely return, she called for her youngest son, Richard, and together the pair removed a wallboard, allowing the child enough access to wedge himself between the interior and exterior walls of the home. Following his placement in the cavity, he was passed the family's silverware, jewelry and currency. Having securely tucked the valuables well beyond arm's reach should the ruse be uncovered, he was removed and the wall board carefully reattached. Her efforts were fruitful, as the house was ransacked later that evening, and much to the disgust of the raiders, not a single item of monetary value was to be found.[241]

The Hendersons were not the exclusive victims of the wrath of the unruly enlisted men, shiftless officers and growing horde of camp followers who had descended on Salisbury. As the sun began to set and local liquor stashes were uncovered, a multitude of other families were preyed upon. Since the vast majority of able-bodied men were in Federal custody, or scattered to the countryside to avoid such a fate, the women of town were left to deal with the increasingly uncomfortable situation. Many were forced to venture through the hostile streets, teeming with intemperate soldiers, to personally request of Stoneman's staff an armed escort for the safety of their family and property.[242]

The former owners of the twins Albert and Victoria, the Bradshaws, were no exception to the sporadic displays of disorder amongst the enlisted men. Upon having their home ransacked and multiple valuables pilfered, the soldiers uncovered a keg of spirits secluded in the rear of the house. Enlisted men and officers alike took turns filling their canteens with the fiery liquid. As word of the unexpected windfall made its way through the command, many other men forced their way into the Bradshaws' home. Of particular concern to the Bradshaws was an inebriated lieutenant who filled and emptied his canteen twice while in their presence.[243]

After the keg was dry, so were the soldiers' interests in the victimized family. While not visited again, Mrs. Bradshaw spent the remainder of the next two days nervously resting on her last valuable possessions and refused to budge from atop her perch, which consisted of a few bags of flour, cornmeal, a side of bacon, a few greens and potatoes. While financially ruined due to the looting, the family would at least have sustenance in the ensuing weeks. Many of their neighbors were not so lucky.[244]

Unfortunately, the plethora of valuables extracted from the local population was not solely confined to the city limits of Salisbury. The disorganized exodus of government stores that were dispatched during the height of the skirmish along Grant's Creek were also targets of Stoneman's ambition. The men of the Eleventh Kentucky were successful in intercepting a train that had departed from Salisbury, bound for some form of refuge farther down the line. Aboard the train were the widow and daughters of the late Confederate general Leonidas Polk, who was killed the previous year defending Atlanta from Sherman.[245]

After the civilians disembarked the train, the personal valuables of the passengers were unloaded and ransacked. The intrinsic valuables were pocketed, and the remainders were burned, along with the government stores that were also aboard. It was there, before the eyes of the grieving widow and the former warrior bishop's daughters, that the general's sword was uncovered in the bottom of a trunk that served as the last resting place of his personal effects. Ecstatic at such a find, the soldiers departed with their martially aesthetic bounty, leaving only a measly collection of token reminders of their dispatched father and husband in the hands of a distraught family.[246]

While there were many notable instances of looting, the men under Stoneman's auspices were rather well behaved in light of what could have transpired. Considering Salisbury was the site of a depot and a notorious prison, Stoneman had more than enough justification to have loosed the dogs of war. In spite of the license that many of his brother officers, including many of his superiors, would have taken in full, a level of civility was maintained by Stoneman, despite the well-documented privations bestowed upon many civilians.[247]

Continuing his standing orders to respect personal property according to the Constitution, the utmost attention was given to make sure that the opportunistic elements of his command respected private property and liberty. However, in a city the size of Salisbury, it is nearly impossible to guarantee that every single soldier would abide these orders when removed from his superiors. Out of eyesight from the more obedient company commanders, it is true that several enlisted men and junior officers took poetic license in what constituted private property during the occupation of Salisbury. Compounded with the copious amount of drink that was found in the city, the lack of chaos that hallmarked the sacking of cities such as Atlanta and Columbia speaks for itself. The peaceful exit of the command was indeed a testament to the diligence of Stoneman's staff and his provost marshals in the execution of their duty.

The reasons behind Stoneman's grace toward a rebellious city that had inflicted so much harm on his compatriots remain a mystery. However, many local legends attempt to explain why the expected razing of the city never occurred. Tales, all of which are unfounded, stress either the relationship of Stoneman to a former schoolmate by the name of Nathaniel Boyden, his involvement in a Masonic pact to save the city or even a common courtesy extended to a local warehouse owner who provided the general room and board for the duration of his stay. While the first two have been disproven by Stoneman's biographer, who noted the erroneous stretch of the imagination to suppose that Stoneman had attended a private boarding school in Massachusetts when his academic career is thoroughly documented and that proof of his Masonic membership had never surfaced, it is interesting to note that the last had some hints of truth behind it.[248]

A local tobacco merchant by the name of T.J. Meroney had entertained Stoneman on the morning of the thirteenth, and at the merchant's request, his warehouse was spared. However, the county courthouse was ordered to be put to the torch. Due to the courthouse's proximity to the warehouse, if the public building was incinerated, the fire would most certainly have spread to the warehouse. After this fact was pointed out by Meroney, Stoneman obliged his host and canceled the burning. Thus, through the opportunistic actions of one local entrepreneur, many valuable court records and infrastructure were saved for the postbellum period.[249]

Aside from the various actions against the inhabitants of the city, the command was very effective in executing its primary goals in Salisbury: the destruction of the prison and the military stores housed at the government complex. Upon completion of the store's inventory, some of which was overseen by Stoneman personally, the general ordered the Confederate property strewn out in the streets for Appalachian camp followers, Negroes, poor whites and prostitutes to cherry pick before the remainder was incinerated. Of the buildings and property that met their doom that afternoon, irreplaceable infrastructure such as a foundry, a distillery, an arsenal and ordnance warehouses were reduced to ashes. Along with the razing of the government's property, the offices and workhouses of the Central and Western Railroads, as well as a private tannery, were touched with fire in an effort to render the dying government impotent in the piedmont.[250]

The raiders inflicted monumental damage to the lost cause with their seizure of the government stores in Salisbury. According to the dispatches of General Gillem, 10,000 stands of arms, 1,000,000 rounds of ammunition, 10,000 artillery projectiles, 6,000 pounds of black powder, 10,000 bushels of corn, 75,000 full sets of uniforms, 250,000 English wool blankets, 20,000 pounds of leather, 6,000 pounds of bacon, 100,000 pounds of salt, 20,000 pounds of sugar, 27,000 pounds of rice, 10,000 pounds of salt peter, 50,000 bushels of wheat, 80 barrels of turpentine, $15,000,000 in Confederate paper money and approximately $100,000 in medical stores were all put to the torch. The supplies that were destroyed were irreplaceable to the bankrupt government, rapidly accelerating the privations faced by the remaining few divisions that elected to fight on. In a very real sense, the last vestiges of hope that any Confederate army that remained in the field clung to went up in flames at Salisbury.[251]

Then there was the much-coveted psychological prize for Stoneman— the prison, over whose liberation he had long salivated. However, much to Stoneman's dismay, the general was once again robbed of his much-coveted title of prison liberator. The prison at Salisbury, which was overcrowded beyond all humanity, had become a morgue for four thousand men due to

The Confederate prison at Salisbury as it appeared in 1863; naturally, this was prior to the hellish overcrowding that came to dominate the affairs of the camp the following year. *Courtesy of the Library of Congress.*

starvation and disease in the short time from September 1864 to February 1865. An issue of particular contention with those who were familiar with the prison were the thousands who were forced to make due with whatever shelter they could find since the prison only had two hundred tents allocated to it. This unfortunate deficiency left the men to live in self-burrowed holes, in spite of the fact that there was an ample supply of timber within eyesight that could have been easily harvested to construct lean-tos.[252]

The situation that developed in Salisbury echoed that of more notorious prison camps, such as Andersonville. While the magnitude of the depredation and death may have differed by location, the root cause was the same. Due to the refusal of the Lincoln administration to adhere to the cartel agreed upon for prisoner exchange, the population of the prison surged from a manageable five thousand to a catastrophic ten thousand men. The official reasoning as to why the great emancipator took this dire route was his protest over the treatment of black combatants at the hands of the Confederates. More realistically, the decision served as an attempt to bleed the Confederate army dry by not sending men south who could once again be placed in the field.[253]

Distraught with the conditions of the prison, presented with the possibility of a prisoner exchange along the coast of North Carolina and fearful of retribution should the city fall into the hands of the Federal army while the prisoners were still present, Governor Zebulon B. Vance ordered the

Former residents of the Salisbury prison on their way to parole in the North. *Courtesy of the Library of Congress.*

prison to be evacuated in late February. On February 22, 1865, the prison at Salisbury was emptied, with the exception of the prisoners who were too infirm to make the overland venture to Raleigh. Upon arrival at the state capital, the prisoners were boarded on rail cars destined for Wilmington. It was there, on March 2, that they received their long-awaited parole papers and left for Northern ports.[254]

Once the majority of its inhabitants were removed, the prison was quickly dissolved as a functioning entity. With numerous Federal bodies traversing the piedmont, the decision was made to abandon the palisades entirely. The remaining five hundred men were shipped to Charlotte only a few days before Stoneman's arrival. Thus, the aspiring liberator was twice denied the title—first at the hands of the Confederates in Georgia and second, by ironic timing in North Carolina. Confronted with the sight of an empty prison, the only consolation for Stoneman was the satisfaction of personally overseeing its destruction. The gratifying work was allocated to the Twelfth Ohio, which undertook its work with an expediency, as one officer remembered, that was actuated by a higher motive than even a just revenge.[255]

Although the city lay open to conquest, the fight for its surrounding infrastructure was far from finished. On the outskirts of the city was a trestle that had been fortified by the efforts of men from the Army of Tennessee under Featherstone at the beginning of the month. On the afternoon of the twelfth, the remaining Confederates in the region were corralled together, ordered to inhabit the defenses and to make a stand on the Davison County side of the Yadkin. No sooner had the earthworks been manned than the troopers of the Third Brigade fell upon them.[256]

The position was commanding, as the Confederate side of the Yadkin provided the defenders with the topographical benefit of a high bluff. This natural advantage was pressed by augmenting the entrenched infantry with an unspecified number of artillery pieces, whose deadly range was increased by the steep incline. While the Third Brigade made a halfhearted attempt to cross the river, the artillery barrage was too intense for the men to successfully force a crossing. Under heavy and determined rifle fire, Miller's men more or less poked and prodded the defenses instead of engaging in an all-out assault against the entrenchments.[257]

Miller's decision not to order a full assault against the bluff was likely due to the fact that the primary objective of rendering Salisbury impotent had been accomplished. Knowing full well that the rail lines were severed in multiple places toward the east, the immediate trestle was consequently incapacitated, and it would have been a tragedy to lose countless lives for a yellow pine structure of little value. In one last attempt to break the Confederate grip on the bluffs, the commander of the Third Brigade ordered the captured artillery brought up from Salisbury. The cannonade was assembled piecemeal, as each piece arrived on the scene one at a time, and continued to thunderously announce their presence in a sporadic fashion until dark. Apparently, their efforts did little good, and the cannonade was ceased after a few hours. Finally, in disgust, the Third Brigade withdrew, leaving the tattered ensemble defending the trestle, with license to claim that it had handed the raiders their only defeat of the entire campaign.[258]

While the men under Stoneman's direct auspices were advancing on Salisbury, the First Brigade, under Palmer, was following a series of roads that took it from its near-miss with the Confederate president at Greensboro to a reunion with the remainder of the division. Although the men of the First Brigade were unaware that Davis was in the town and that they had come within only a few thousand feet of capturing the renegade president, the proximity of the Federal cavalry was enough to encourage Beauregard and Johnston to demand that the president exit North Carolina for a safer environment—an undertaking that Davis began on April 14. Oblivious to the course of events that their presence near Greensboro had set into motion, during the heat of the day of the twelfth, a very fatigued First Brigade rode into Salisbury and instantly fell out into camp for a much-deserved night of rest.[259]

As the clock struck three on the afternoon of April 13, the reunified command departed Salisbury. Large segments of the industrial center were still engulfed in flames, and materials from the arsenal were sporadically exploding at points throughout the compound—a phenomenon that haunted the inhabitants of the city for several days to come. With the body reunited and its primary objectives complete, the troopers of Stoneman's command began their leisurely ascent back into the spires of the Blue Ridge. Elated with the command's role in bringing the conflict to a close, and with his martial reputation intact, Stoneman was content to withdraw his brigades back to the safe haven of East Tennessee. While perhaps Asheville, Charlotte and Statesville warranted visitation on his return trip to Knoxville, in the New Yorker's mind, the raid was functionally over. However, developments that originated in Danville would keep Stoneman's tired men in the saddle for the next two months and send them deeper into the South than anyone could have foreseen when the command first made its frigid decent from the Appalachian Mountains in late March.[260]

"You Can See Murder on the Face of It"

The infernal racket of the mockingly monotonous tick produced by the brass table clock's internal mechanisms seemed almost synchronized with his throbbing pain, as if it were a metronome pacing Old Scratch himself through this opus of agony. The grueling torment that had commandeered the lounging sufferer's entire being had slowly been brewing in his body for days. The rolling perspiration that cascaded down his weathered brow, plunged from the sudden precipice at the extremes of the sharp cheeks under the weary eyes and reabsorbed into the mangled beard below was not indicative of the temperature in the room. Instead, it signified the tension produced by a rattled nervous system, which had twice been beaten into a dulled submission, only to be driven to the point of reanimation by the insistent onslaught of pain throughout the course of one of the longest nights of the wounded man's life.

Then there was the imminent danger, an unavoidable conundrum that tormented his subconscious. Knowing full well that any gurgle in his stomach would herald an appointment that would result in an unspeakably searing tear in the most private of areas, the general unbuttoned his fly in an effort to give the previous night's dinner room to ferment in his tract without forcing the issue. Well aware that there was no room for breakfast to be crammed into an already densely packed colon, the tactician elected to enjoy coffee at Meroney's table while his staff consumed warm plates full of the merchant's hospitality. Upon vacating the dining room, the sensation of pressure against his bladder alerted the ailing officer that this demonstration in gratitude was quickly turning into a fatal error.

It was nigh on a handful of minutes until noon, and George Stoneman could hear the harmony of the boisterous commands projected from various sergeants resonating through the streets of Salisbury, sailing into his chamber through an open window as the entire division prepared to embark on a route that the suffering old trooper was still trying to decide in this late hour. Understanding that his natural course of return would take him westward to Statesville, the conundrum rested in which gap through the Blue Ridge to utilize. This decision was made increasingly unpleasant as sharp spikes of pain originating in his derrière fettered his concentration. The difficulty of the task increased as the weary soldier was forced to lie on his back, and the burdensome toll of gravity made any attempt to keep a map taut above his eyes futile.

"Goddamn these piles!" The curse was less stated than bemoaned with a sigh as the general came to the realization of what the day ahead held for his infirmity. "I can't mount, it will not be an hour before my trousers are soaked in blood." Running unobstructed through the peculiar process that resides within the tactical mind, Stoneman weighed his options and their inevitable consequences. "It is a shame that after traveling all these miles and finally experiencing a fortunate campaign, I'm struck crippled by this damned ailment." Concentrating on the excruciating throbbing as blood forced its way through the constricted mounds of flesh, the grieving soul lamented further, "There is no possible way to position myself in the saddle that will bring any semblance of relief." Knowing full well that he could not rest his command in Salisbury due to the looming possibility of Beauregard arriving in strength to retake the city, the weeklong reprieve that would be needed for his hemorrhoids to subside was not a luxury even the injured could consider.[261]

Scrounging for the resolve to face the crippling disadvantage of his infirmity, the enfeebled officer elevated his torso by resting on his elbows, gave his throat a deep cleaning signified by the gruff shuffle of a reverberating Adam's apple and bellowed toward the door left ajar that led to the next room, where unseen officers were preparing dispatches. Within a matter of seconds, the door swung fully open on its hinges. Standing before the general was a captain, in a brushed yet still dusty uniform, with his weight laid predominately against the doorknob, exercising the liberty that forgoes the traditional snap to attention afforded those who were at the tail end of a hard-ridden campaign. Casting his eyes on the deservedly stoop-shouldered captain, Stoneman instructed the junior officer to set into motion the procurement of a buggy with a frame limber enough to absorb the agonizingly jarring blows that would inevitably ensue as the command made its way up the rocky mountain roads. Left alone with his thoughts following the swift exit of the captain, the discomfited general resumed the contemplative chore of weighing the advantages and liabilities of the various avenues that led into Tennessee.

Shortly after three o'clock that afternoon, a feeble Stoneman descended the front steps of the Meroney home, struggling to maintain proper posture in an attempt to conceal his agonizing weakness from his men—even though every step generated a repetitive friction that inflamed his lower body. Continuing the charade as the humbled officer negotiated the footstones of the front walk, his deep, stone-cold eyes concentrated on the japanned metallic steps of a modestly expensive buggy halted at the front of the home. Taking deep and deliberate breaths in a vain attempt at mental preparation for the commanding task at hand, the general pressed his left hand against the carriage, which bestowed the weight of his body on the vehicle to such an extent that the buggy rocked on its springs.[262]

Slowly elevating his right foot, the tormented traveler took a deep sigh, as if resigning himself to a prison sentence, at the very moment he transferred the weight of his body from the walk path to the black metallic steps and elevated himself with the power of his quivering right leg. Letting loose a cough while his body left the earth in an attempt to disguise the grimace that had engulfed the weary face concealed under the shroud of a long, wiry beard, the general thrust his left leg into the carriage proper, facilitating a desperate lunge at the rear bench seat. This silently heroic effort would have most likely resulted in the ailing officer's tumble into the floorboard were it not for the quick reaction of his right hand, which bolted forward to stoutly bear his collapsing body against the opposite wall of the fuselage.

Bracing his wretched body with the palms of both hands pressed firmly against the rear wooden bench of the carriage, the sufferer lowered his swollen buttock onto the smooth pine boards. Glaring at the empty bench opposite, a sigh of relief deeply coursed through his nostrils. It was at that point that an unexpected object caught the attention of his right peripheral—a red velvet pillow that had been mockingly placed against the exit wall of the carriage. Shame crept up from his loins and overwhelmed his entire body as the realization crashed down on him that his private aliments were anything but. Stoneman fully extended his right leg, shifted his weight strategically upon the opposing hip and violently grabbed at the pillow with his near arm. Shifting the majority of weight to the left side of his body, the sufferer swiftly slid the pillow into position under his ailment as to avoid further irritation.

No sooner had the silent laborer secured a position that was relatively acceptable to his ailment than all illusion of privacy was violated by the entrance of his chief of staff and a solitary private into the carriage. With nothing more than a resigned look of defeat in his eyes, the pair was made thoroughly uncomfortable by the torment that their superior was experiencing. Devoid of verbal expression, the pair secured an embarrassedly conscious placement on the bench opposite their commander as the chief of staff opened a satchel to pantomime the inspection of delicate papers that resided within, while the private placed his Spencer carbine between his feet and inspected the length of the weapon in silence. The close of the carriage door by some unseen external attendant signaled to the driver that the journey was underway, and the buggy jolted forward as the team pulled away to accompany the column leaving Salisbury.

While the gallop of the team rocked the carriage to and fro down the streets of the sacked city, Stoneman instantly lamented his decision to passively leave his conquest in the secluded privacy offered by the enclosed vehicle; it was a proud moment, and his rightful place was at the head of the column. But as the carriage began to hurdle the imbedded rocks that were intermittently uncovered by years of erosion in the roadbed that led to Statesville, the foresight of the general's decision became all too clear. Even with the insulation afforded by four reinforced wheels, it seemed as if it would only be a matter of time before one of his strategically placed pustules would rupture. In the midst of Stoneman's lion hour, he was, in fact, as feeble as a kitten.

As the column left Salisbury and lightheartedly trekked westerly toward Statesville, word of its movements began to spread across the region. With tales of countless mules and horses being pilfered from the countryside homes that rested between the two cities arriving among the frantically bustling populace, the residents of Statesville spent the morning of April 13 in earnest dread, as logic dictated that Stoneman's men would descend on their town with a ravenous appetite. They were not to be disappointed.

Possessing the foresight to post two sentries selected from among the trustworthy men of the town a half dozen miles down the road in the direction of Salisbury, the inhabitants of Statesville sought to provide themselves with ample warning to prepare for the inevitable visitation. Through the early afternoon, valuables were collected from most of the inhabitants of the town and stored in strategically out-of-the-way locations. Following the tedious security of the heavy wealth, the men of the town filled their pockets with intrinsic valuables and collected enough provender for the handful of days they would need to lay low in the surrounding forest in an attempt to avoid capture should the Union troopers elect to undertake a prolonged occupation of the small town.[263]

Somewhere in the neighborhood of early evening, the two scouts dispatched by the nervous townsfolk, J.S. Miller and T.A. Watts, rode into Statesville at a full gallop and reported to the populace that the advance scouts of a Union command had arrived at the point they chose to observe them—a mere six miles from the town limits. Following the utterance of the dreadful developments, an organized exodus of the male population from the town commenced. The stalwarts of the paternalist Southern hierarchy fled into the woods in small groups, abandoning the fabled convictions of masculinity that had been instilled in every fiber of their being since the earliest memories took root in their minds, lest they join the ever-growing trail of prisoners accompanying Stoneman's column on its return trip to Knoxville. The end result of the mass flight of machismo was that the town of Statesville was almost exclusively inhabited by women and young children by the time the blue troopers began to melt into the city limits.[264]

The foresight of the town's male citizens to abandon their homes in the name of self-preservation had been much warranted. Stoneman's various brigades were fraught with a propensity for taking prisoners by the time they had left Salisbury, and just as when the command left Virginia, they were followed by a long line of legitimate prisoners and several martial kidnappings disguised in an effort to weed out saboteurs. As the advance guard rode into Statesville, it was abundantly clear that the dusty blue veterans had no intention of making a genteel acquaintance with the population. In a similar entrance to that of Salisbury, the troopers exploded onto the streets of Statesville firing weapons into the air and quickly secured the town blocks by splintering companies into squads and establishing picket posts throughout the town. By the time twilight passed on the night of April 13, Statesville was locked down, and anyone found on the streets was immediately placed under arrest for interrogation by a very exhausted provost martial.[265]

The command trickled into Statesville piecemeal in a long, dust-shrouded parade that lasted well into the early morning hours. The citizens of the town anxiously watched the ghastly earth-covered phantoms jostle into town, very much afraid of what their presence signified. However, the weary riders passed through town without incident and bivouacked on the grounds of the local college. The men who arrived on the night of the thirteenth belonged to the Second and Third Brigades, as once again Stoneman's warhorse, the First Brigade, had been dispatched to render the railroad lines west of Statesville useless and to feint an acceptable distance toward the city of Charlotte.[266]

Following the lockdown of the city and the arrival of Stoneman at Statesville, orders for selective destruction were handed out to subordinate officers from the agitated New Yorker. It was at this point that the town's depot was razed, and the Confederate stores that resided within were divided up amongst the train of white Appalachian camp followers and the self-emancipated blacks who accompanied the command into the borough. One act of destruction that appeared out of the ordinary was the dictated destruction of the printing press and offices of a local circulation known as the *Iredell Express*. Upon discovery that the publishing house was to be put to the torch, local citizens pled for its pardon due to the immense contribution that the periodical bestowed on the common good.[267]

However, these earnest pleas fell on deaf ears. In an act of desperation, the few male citizens who remained in town offered their assistance in the demolition of the building, pleading permission to further pile the wreckage in an open space that could serve as an orderly bonfire and would not threaten any other adjoining buildings, thus preventing the spark that could lead to a citywide fire. Upon refusal of this generous proposal laid before the officer who oversaw the destruction of the building housing the press, it was sparked and quickly engulfed in flames. Much to the prophetic fear of the townspeople, the home of Dr. Y.S. Dean was incinerated following the inferno that engulfed the press.[268]

Physical destruction of the last remnants of the Confederacy appeared to not be the only motive of Stoneman's visit to the region. Multiple historians have theorized that the old New Yorker may have engaged in a string of beneficial manumissions while traveling through the farmland surrounding Statesville. Stoneman, a democrat New Yorker who, on more than one occasion, referred to contraband slaves as a hindrance to the progress of cavalry, apparently encouraged male slaves to abandon their role of servitude in the fields of the Piedmont South and depart with his army. Not taking into account that separation from their families could have monumentally disastrous effects on the men he was recruiting for the cause of the Union, Stoneman's intentions appear to have been motivated by the fact that the general was trying to break the last vestiges of moral and antebellum culture amongst the slaveholding population. In the old trooper's mind, by forcing the former operators to engage in manual labor, a degree of humility could possibly be instilled in the defeated male population.[269]

The command's decision to venture into the area encompassing Statesville was not solely due to the natural course of geography, but it was also a result of practical intentions. Drawing supplies from the various Confederate stores cached at the most quintessential cities of the western Piedmont, coupled with the scouring of the countryside and hamlets for acceptable mounts, Stoneman's command was sufficiently supplied for its return trek up the summit of the Blue Ridge by April 14. The general himself went as far as to exclaim that his men were better mounted than they had been at the start of their venture. The end result was the ability to supply approximately one thousand contrabands with mounts, and many members of his prisoner train were atop acceptable beasts in an effort to expedite their return to Tennessee. The adventure to the Piedmont had indeed been a fruitful one.[270]

Knowing full well that the First Brigade was bound for Statesville and only a few solitary miles from closing the gap with its sister brigades, Stoneman reflected on the accomplishments of his raid. The early week's efforts of destroying the Virginia and Tennessee Railroad, severing any viable line of retreat for the Army of Northern Virginia; the destruction of priceless war goods; the razing of the empty prison at Salisbury in the closing days of the raid; the destruction of dozens of irreplaceable infrastructures around the region; and the instillation of fretful anxiety amongst the Confederate populace were warranted laurels crowning the success of the campaign. Knowing that little more could be done to aid in the destruction of the rebellion, Stoneman outlined plans for return to his home base and the command's strategic relocation in Western North Carolina to prevent the unlikely development of a guerrilla movement in the region.[271]

Encouraged by his ailment, Stoneman met with the advance guard of the First Brigade and left orders for Palmer to press on toward Lincolnton following their arrival in Statesville to monitor the north bank of the Catawba River. In conjunction with the fate of the First, the Second and Third Brigades were to be rereleased to their original commander, General Gillem, and were ordered to progress on to Asheville in an effort to occupy the urban heart of Appalachian North Carolina, with the intention of troubleshooting any difficulty that might develop in the closing weeks of the war. Engrossed in the satisfaction of a campaign well served, Stoneman, in turn, would return to his headquarters in Knoxville with the prisoners and contrabands through the most direct route that could be uncovered.[272]

Early on the morning of the fourteenth, the Second and Third Brigades accompanied Stoneman on his exodus from Statesville. For a few hours, the fretful population could breathe a sigh of relief in hopes that normalcy would return. However, about midnight, the First Brigade arrived and occupied the abandoned campsite in which the remainder of the division had laid their heads the evening before. Having completed grueling consecutive sidebars that took a greater toll on the soldiers who made up the First Brigade than on those of the other two brigades, Palmer elected to rest his men for two full days. While some local lore records episodes of looting and even beatings at the hands of the Second and Third Brigades, once again Palmer's true Northern men appeared to have maintained a very professional presence in Statesville.[273]

While Palmer's unfortunate men were busy trying to recoup their sore mounts and battered bodies, their rest was far from undisturbed. A detachment of Ferguson's Cavalry, led by Lieutenant A.B. Coffee, launched a surprise charge against Palmer's pickets during a lull in their attention. Although the source of much alarm, the charge was repulsed without a single Union casualty—a vain action that witnessed Lieutenant Coffee shot from his mount and killed prior to the uncontested withdrawal of his men. The deflection of the detachment stirred up a hornets' nest, as the various rogue Confederate cavalry elements that inhabited the region descended on Statesville. By the time the First Brigade withdrew on the morning of the seventeenth, it had grown accustomed to the sporadic nips by diminutive bands of cavalry that either sought to probe Palmer's defenses for some semblance of advantage or rode blindly into Statesville assuming it to be an open city devoid of any Union presence.[274]

The latter holds a semblance of truth. Following the desertion of Statesville by Palmer for a more bountiful destination in Lincolnton, two Confederate regiments limped into the town and bivouacked, much to the delight of the shaken citizenry. Euphoric elation, however, was not the emotion warranted for such a development. Decrepit and ornery, this tattered rabble in no way embodied the mounted saviors or chivalric knights long idealized as a cornerstone of antebellum Southern culture. Instead, the mismatched and stoop-shouldered scarecrows draped in tattered jean had not the regal manes of princely Confederate lions; the harsh reality was that they donned blood-stained, gnarled sheep's hide that thinly veiled the wolves from the unsuspecting flock.[275]

As in other towns where Stoneman's command was shadowed by overwhelmed and impotent Confederate elements, the regiments of both Vaughn and Wheeler descended on Statesville with disastrous results. Following their securing of the town and the establishment of picket posts, wayward Confederate troopers turned on the citizens they were charged to protect. Exploiting the confusion shrouding the late hours of the war, apathetic officers consumed with illusions of survival and a judicial cavity created by a country locked in its death throes, the majority of troopers from the Deep South began to loot the town to a degree that would have shamed the best efforts of their adversaries. In one notorious instance, fifty bales of cotton were put to the torch because they were the surviving property of speculators whom the embittered men believed in their battered hearts were profiteering off the troopers' misery at the front—a clear sign that many of the remaining soldiers in the Confederate army had come to understand the classist nature of their war effort.[276]

The First Brigade's procession to Lincolnton was short, covering the forty-odd miles that separated the two locales in short order. As the sun commenced its lengthy return trip toward the western horizon on April 17, the advance guard of the command arrived at what one veteran of the raid later recalled as a town inhabited by a populace that was extremely and bitterly rebellious. Visibility was impaired as dust generated by the evaporation of the morning's moisture from the warmth of midday was kicked up along the road into Lincolnton by countless hooves repeatedly stamping the pulverized soil. It was under this visual disadvantage that earth-encrusted troopers fell victim to a long-anticipated, yet rarely witnessed, occurrence.[277]

A cool circulation of air, indicative of the nerve-shattering sensation generated by a missed appointment with a sniper's bullet tauntingly caressed the shoulder of General Palmer as he rode within sight of the town housing about one thousand inhabitants, thus validating the extremes of the population's disgust for the troopers. Following the alarming dissection of the dusty air by the unseen projectile, Palmer ordered his staff and Company E of the Fifteenth Pennsylvania forward to root out the veiled assailant. Vaulting from his poorly concealed position in the early spring greenery like a startled hare, the aspiring sniper stretched his legs frantically across the developing straw of the field in a desperate attempt to reach the refuge of the tree line. His legs, no matter how hard they were thrust into the warm blades of grass, could not outpace the well-mounted troopers, resulting in his swift corral by the infuriated recipients of his marksmanship. Demanding to face the man who had the audacity to fire the cowardly shot upon his unsuspecting column, Palmer ordered the suspect brought before him.[278]

Standing fully erect, as a twitching eyelid fluttered by the unseen hand of a puppeteer known as hatred, the general was taken aback by what his senses laid before him. The assailant who had attempted to dispatch the unsuspecting Quaker was not a man at all but a mere boy—smooth faced and hardly into the heart of his teenage seasons. Face to face with the officer he attempted to dispatch, the frightened youth could barely muster the strength to confront the burning hatred residing in the general's eyes, much less attempt to defend or justify his actions. The awkwardness of the conundrum served to temper Palmer's raging anger and abate his appetite for revenge.[279]

In due expedience, the mother of the aspiring bushwhacker arrived on the scene to plead for mercy on her son's behalf. Clearly distraught at the fanatical display of bravado at the hands of her offspring, she pleaded for his safe return to their home. The heartfelt petition for lenience was founded on the reassurance that the youth would be anything but a nuisance in the presence of the brigade. Palmer grudgingly accepted, forcing the constricting lump of revenge down his throat in a hard-felt swallow, and afterward the freshman bushwhacker was released to his mother on the condition that he would not be seen by the offended officer again.[280]

Benevolence, however, did not reduce the local population's sudden affinity for the malevolent art of bushwhacking. As Palmer's men bedded down for the night in preparation for the next morning's adventures, the brigade cautiously established picket posts at strategic locations throughout the vicinity of Lincolnton. One of the soldiers thrust to the fringes of the ominous shadows of the night, a corporal by the name of George French, was advising his detail as to the evening's task when he was cut down by a bushwhacker's bullet erupting from a mysterious position. It was the first death that the command had experienced in several days, and in this late hour of the war, it did not sit well with the troopers.[281]

Fearing a demoniacal reprisal, the Episcopal Church in town immediately donated a plot in its cemetery to serve as the final resting place of the slain corporal. Following the completion of the morbid ceremony, local women attempted to placate the troopers further by decorating the freshly broken earth with a multitude of arranged flower displays harvested from the patches dotting Lincolnton. Wary that the fiery tempers of the occupying soldiers over the cowardly termination of their compatriot's life were not entirely cooled, the town made an effort to become increasingly hospitable toward their unwelcomed guest. Many of the prominent citizens in the town invited officers and enlisted men alike to dinner at their residences, while many of the house servants were put to work preparing breads, biscuits and pies for those not fortunate enough to warrant an invitation to the warm abodes.[282]

Unfortunately for the weary troopers, time did not accommodate a proper exploitation of the explosion of good will. The First Brigade was dispatched to the humble town with a task at hand and on the morning of the eighteenth, preparations were made to execute the first phase of Stoneman's post-raid designs. With morning roll call and various officers' meetings completed, the brigade was strategically fragmented. By midmorning, the carefully arranged splinters were loosed upon the countryside, all released with an assigned task to undertake, and at the center of it all, Lincolnton served as the headquarters for the seemingly lengthy operation.

The Fifteenth Pennsylvania drew the luxurious privilege of holding the headquarters at Lincolnton, a rare glimmer of fortune in contrast to the hard riding that the regiment had come to expect throughout much of the raid. However, the windfall of idleness was not shared equally throughout the regiment, as a battalion of men under Major Wagner was dispatched to the countryside in an excursion to collect suitable replacements for its depleted mounts. The equally exhausted and less fortunate regiments, the Tenth Michigan and the Twelfth Ohio, were ordered to follow the railroad tracks to the Catawba River and scout the situation along its banks. In addition to their surveillance of the river, the regiments were ordered to render any infrastructure found along the way useless to the local population.[283]

The morning was not without its occurrences. The estranged battalion from the Fifteenth Pennsylvania rode into the farmland that snaked along the rocky Catawba River, only to draw the day's warm action. It was there, lounging in the shade of the trees that dipped their roots into the banks of the rolling Catawba, that the battalion surprised a camp of local home guardsmen who had been burdened with orders to protect the bridge that spanned the river. Feathers still ruffled from the audacity of the previous day's bushwhacking, the battalion charged headlong into its adversaries.[284]

The startled amateur combatants did not provide much opposition to the challenge thrust upon them by the sudden arrival of a battalion of hardened Federal troopers. Startled, the inhabitants of the camp quickly melted into the trees after only firing a few untrained shots. Following the scattering, Wagner ordered his men to sort through the camp and to burn the bridge that was so ineptly defended by the local elders. The structure was reduced to cinders before the afternoon's heat had settled in, and with time to spare, Wagner took it upon himself to destroy a mile of track on his return trip to Lincolnton.[285]

With the local rails rendered useless on what the troopers hoped would be the first day of light occupation duty, the morning of the nineteenth brought yet another reprieve from the fast-paced overland marathon scramble that had signified the previous few weeks. The three regiments were splintered into fragments that ranged in size from a detail to a full company. Dispatched throughout the countryside in an effort to round up the remnants of the local home guard, which contemporary records contend may have comprised as many as 225 armed men roving the woods waiting for an opportunity to bushwhack an unsuspecting trooper, no stone was left unturned in Lincoln County.[286]

Seeking out the last remnants of infrastructure beneficial to the expiring Confederate cause, Major Wagner led an expedition to the Vesuvius Iron Furnace that towered over one of the largest properties in the county. Along the meandering path that led to the targeted forge, many unfortunate persons were arrested in a continued effort to curtail the threat of bushwhacking. Upon arriving at the furnace, Wagner elected to parole his prisoners instead of maintaining them—a move that was becoming increasingly more common following the capitulation of the Army of Northern Virginia ten days earlier. As the parole reached its completion, Wagner allowed his men an opportunity to entertain their curiosity about the iron furnace that stood in the background of the emasculation. Two men went as so far as to light its fire and provide the curious interlopers with a demonstration of how the mammoth chimney operated.[287]

The patronizingly generous paroles were not exclusive to the prisoners who were under the charge of Major Wagner. In all, approximately eight hundred unfortunate souls, whose ill fortune brought them across the command's path, were paroled in the vicinity of Lincolnton. Although hundreds of prisoners had been sent over the mountains bound for Ohio in the early days of the raid, martial evolution took hold, and the changing nature of the war made such migratory ventures an exercise in excessiveness. With the First Brigade anchored at Lincolnton and anointed with the duty of suppressing potential guerrilla threats, the paroling of prisoners locally by Palmer's men served to both identify potential bushwhackers and to extend the first olive branch of good will toward a conquered people.[288]

While the parolees were being executed throughout the county, Palmer was presented with the grand information that he had long hoped to receive, albeit from a very unlikely source. Midafternoon on April 19, three Confederate troopers rode into Lincolnton under a flag of truce, clutching a message penned by the hand of General Sherman. The order outlined the developments that were transpiring near Durham, North Carolina, and that the two opposing theater commanders had agreed to halt their campaigns in an impromptu armistice. Aside from the directive to cease all hostilities instantly, the entire division was ordered to ride out for Durham, employing the utmost expedience, in an effort to link up with Sherman's army in order to consolidate all Federal resources in the likely event that a lengthy occupation of the region was needed.[289]

However, not all of the news delivered by the Rebel messengers was joyous. The gray-clad envoys also unfolded the tragic tale of the assassination of President Lincoln and the startling manhunt for his dispatcher. The looks that hung on the beleaguered faces of the soldiers must have surely dissuaded any plots hatched by the aspiring bushwhackers intermixed with the local populace of Lincolnton. The cold stares radiating from the steely eyes of the disenchanted troopers surely gave the impression that if any misstep was made by even a solitary citizen at this painful hour, the town would be reduced to rubble.[290]

Wasting no time, Palmer dispatched a series of riders to ascertain the location of his sister brigades, hoping that they possessed further information about the location of the rendezvous point for the trek to Durham. It was at this juncture that the destiny of the command became ambiguous. Troopers from an unmentioned source arrived in Lincolnton bearing orders that the First Brigade disavow the directive originating from the central counties of the state. Instead, Palmer was to make ready to move his regiments toward a reunion with the remainder of the command, which had just been ordered the previous evening to advance over the Blue Ridge Mountains to Knoxville for a consolidation of force in East Tennessee under General George H. Thomas.[291]

The relative ease and tranquility experienced by the First Brigade following their departure from Statesville was not shared by the other regiments of the command. The journey from Statesville was an uninterrupted ride performed at a frantic pace much akin to their experiences in Virginia and the northern border counties of North Carolina. Driven by an urgent desire for a return to Knoxville, in order to seek relief from his debilitating ailment, Stoneman steered the portion of the command that accompanied him in the direction of Lenoir. As a result of their haste, on the afternoon of the fourteenth, Stoneman and Gillem's Division arrived on the outskirts of Taylorsville.[292]

It was at his makeshift headquarters in the sleepy hamlet that a deserter from the Army of Northern Virginia by the name of Marshall Walker, who had been captured by a scouting detail as he attempted to slip past the halted command at Statesville, informed Stoneman that he had opted to abandon his post near Danville after being informed that the army had been surrendered to Grant. Knowing that the war was now in its twilight hours, Stoneman spared the supply stores in the town and only elected to destroy Confederate court records. There are few, if any, recorded instances of the sporadic looting that had come to characterize a visitation by the Second and Third Brigades while they were halted in Taylorsville. However, one local tradition remembers an aborted attempt by a handful of licentious soldiers to pilfer a family's silverware.[293]

Utilizing a top sheet untucked from a nearby bed, which had metamorphosed into a functional sack through a process of knotting the corners and cinching the linen symmetrically, the family's valuables cascaded into it in a continuous stream fed by the troopers who diligently ransacked the home. As silverware plummeted into the makeshift satchel, an unexpected garment stalked the ornate coinage into the bag. Upon turning the sheepskin face forward, it was apparent that the mystery article was a finely illustrated Masonic apron. The soldier who clutched the sacred garb in his hands, the senior-most enlisted man in the room, ordered all his fellow riders out of the bedchamber without question. It was at that point that the eastern traveler scattered the contents of the billow onto the floor and exited the house in disgust, determined to fulfill his obligation of posting a guard at the door of an unknown brother.[294]

With the war rapidly approaching its conclusion and his ailments abounding, George Stoneman elected to halt the command at Taylorsville for over twenty-four hours in an effort to get a better handle on his affairs. The increasingly large procession of prisoners that accompanied his column was instructed to seek respite in the open air of the courthouse square, under

As the less disciplined elements of the command made their way through the Blue Ridge, they were indiscriminate in their pillage, going so far as to inflict undue hardship on the impoverished elements of the region, despite their separation from the plantation aristocracy. *Courtesy of the Library of Congress.*

strict orders not to meander, lest they were subject to capital punishment. In stark contrast to the exposure experienced by his prize, the enfeebled general took up a posh residence in the opulent McIntosh home, a family of local notables. While Stoneman lamented his feebleness, the village of Taylorsville held its breath in anticipation of the evening to come.[295]

While the infrastructure of the town was spared the indiscriminate judgment cast by the torch, the imposition of burden was not entirely foreign to the nervous population. Brooding in his sore disposition, Stoneman ordered the local women to feed his command. The matrons of Taylorsville were ordered to exude provender for their visitors by drawing from their already depleted food stores, eventually given license to spare whatever they could sacrifice for the prisoners in the courthouse square after the appetites of the command's members had been abated. Exhausted and overwhelmed, local tradition holds that some studious women boiled eggs throughout the course of the day as the ravenous troopers feasted at the foot of their hearths in mechanical shifts.[296]

After a daylong reprieve, Stoneman ordered his command to advance farther west to the rolling lands that cradled the hamlet of Lenoir, a destination that the saddle-weary troopers approached in the late afternoon hours of Easter Sunday 1865. Apathetic to the importance that the day held in the hearts of the inhabitants of the Yadkin Valley, the agitated commander elected to utilize the resources of St. James Episcopal Church in spite of what other activities might have been planned for that evening. Establishing his headquarters in the rectory, the cavalcade of prisoners was confined within the grounds of the graveyard. The short distance traveled by the command on the holiest day of the Christian calendar suggests that Stoneman found himself in the throes of a bloody flare up of his piles and thus was not in his sharpest frame of mind—which abided a minor tactical mistake that could have greatly hampered his fellow officers in East Tennessee should the speculative guerrilla movement arise. The decision to allow civilians to feed his growing collection of prisoners without direct supervision by members of the command afforded an audacious luxury to local philanthropists. This unchecked intermixing with the captives cost the throbbing general knowledge of a very valuable prisoner, upon whom he had unknowingly placed his hands when the division took Salisbury.[297]

In a desperate attempt to launch a preemptive attack against a feared invasion by "Home Yankee" commander George Kirk, who, under orders from General Thomas, had erected a palisade near Blowing Rock to guarantee that Stoneman's command had an unobstructed avenue of escape should events on the raid go sour, Major A.C. Avery ventured from Burke County to Salisbury in an effort to secure much-needed reinforcements from Beauregard in a proposed assault against Kirk's fortresses. However, upon completion of his journey down the winding roads of the Blue Ridge, Salisbury was assaulted by Stoneman's command, and the unattached major was rounded up as just another anonymous prisoner at the Battle of Grant's Creek. Without a designated command, the senior officer was thrown into the general prisoner population without so much as interrogation.[298]

Instantly recognized by local familiars, who in turn understood the real danger of the middle-aged notable being sent to the likes of Camp Chase upon identification, the major was pulled to the side and told to pantomime a conversation with his face turned away from the guard post. In a few moments, other accomplices, aware of the ruse, arrived with a razor, soap and tattered clothing. With a reduction of facial hair that would have broken his heart in less pressing times, the major quickly cleaved his whiskers and shaved his face clean of even the closest semblance of stubble. Following the facial readjustment, a quick devolution in attire cemented his transformation to such an extent that Major Avery was even a stranger amongst those who actually knew him before he donned the gray uniform.[299]

As with the personal character of the war, the definition of what constituted a combatant and hospitable treatment of prisoners changed from brigade to brigade. While Palmer and the First Brigade took liberties in rounding up local men and boys to stave the tide of a potential guerrilla movement, unlike their comrades in arms, the mass herding of the regional male population masked as prisoners was one option for which the Northern volunteers did not have the stomach. After their arrival in Lincolnton and the establishment of a headquarters, paroling the prisoners appeared to be the order of the day.[300]

However, the same benevolence was not common in the Second and Third Brigades. The majority of the prisoners who accompanied Stoneman into Lenoir were unfortunate home guardsmen or bystanders who garnered the malevolence of the troopers. Many of those who accompanied the ghastly trail of weary souls into the town were men who had surpassed military age by the better part of two decades. Furthermore, those found under arms were either captured fleeing uneventful exchanges, such as the fiasco at Grant's Creek, or at stationary assignments that better suited their decrepitly aging bodies.[301]

In spite of their origins or ailing conditions, these prisoners were ordered to march upwards of eight hours a day, traversing twenty-five miles or more a day on their frail feet. Respect for their captives demonstrated by the troopers under Gillem's auspices was not of the caliber that the First Brigade had demonstrated. Inmates were ordered to lie prone at night, deprived of sustenance or the privacy to evacuate, and any man who showed any promise for flight was ordered shot at the first instance of inconvenience to the guards. The treatment of the vanquished, whether through malice or practicality, at the hands of the Second and Third Brigades added exponential fuel to the fire that forged the devilish image of the command in infamy.[302]

The entire definition and tone of the raid dramatically transformed on the morning of April 17. Following a breakfast served in the rectory of the St. James Episcopal Church, Stoneman informed Gillem that his ailment made the trip too miserable to continue. Stoneman had come to the unfortunate conclusion that his disorder had not only become a personal liability but also endangered the remainder of the command. Harkening back to his experiences in Georgia during the previous year, the general was fearful that the slower pace of progression to Tennessee might possibly allow the dying Confederate army time to rally an effective counterattack against a stalled body that had elected to sit idly by while its commander recovered with his pants literally down around his ankles.[303]

It was at that gestation, while Stoneman most likely sipped coffee as his underlings stuffed their gullets at the expense of the local populace, that the old New Yorker informed the ill-tempered Tennessean that he was once again in command of the destiny of his division. Furthermore, by sunset, the triumphant general would depart under the accompaniment of a light escort, the contrabands and notable prisoners. Understanding that such a conclusion was inevitable, the look on Gillem's face was surely that of muted elation, as he knew that the morning's disclosure translated to the fact that he would finally be free to undertake the persona of the warrior he always imagined himself to be—the true embodiment of what General Sherman called "total warfare."

The route that Stoneman elected to employ took him along a series of roads that primarily followed the Yadkin River into Watauga County, scampering along a stagecoach turnpike that constituted the most direct passage into Tennessee. His return trek took the absentee commander directly into the territory that Kirk had secured for him, following the fortified pass at Blowing Rock and on to Boone before crossing the crest of the Blue Ridge Mountains. The thoughts that raced through the old soldier's mind must have been a combination of elation and regret. His elation for the final arrival of a long-eluded laurel earned on an independent campaign was tempered by the regret that the victorious general had to depart at the apex of glory in such an embarrassing, though hidden, circumstance. Despite whatever mysteries existed in the recesses of Stoneman's subconscious, one thing was for certain: the discipline that governed Stoneman's command severely deteriorated following his unheralded departure from the column.[304]

The first sign of what was to come surfaced in Morganton. Alleviated from the encumbrance wrought by his relegation to subordinated commander under Stoneman, Gillem set out for the unsuspecting town with dripping chops. There to whet his appetite further was a minor force of Confederates positioned squarely in the middle of his line of march at the Rocky Ford on the Catawba River. Ragged and defeated, yet somehow still compelled to make a stand, the force, which stood at about battalion strength, was reinforced with a solitary piece of artillery and led by Confederate major general John Porter McCown.[305]

The three hundred Confederate diehards collided with the raiders approximately two and a half miles from Morganton, huddling in the ready-made fortifications that surrounded the bridge after loosing implements of destruction on its wooden floorboards—a tactic eerily reminiscent of the engagement at Grant's Creek on the outskirts of Salisbury. Understanding that the Rebels intended to withdraw to the opposing bank, thus drawing the troopers deeper into the narrow crossing in an attempt to facilitate a slaughter, Gillem ordered the position flanked by crossing the Catawba upstream from the entrenchments. A large contingent of the Eighth Tennessee under the guidance of Major Christopher Kenner forded the river two miles above the defenses and moved behind the defenders, completing encirclement unbeknownst to General McCown. A second battalion from the Eighth drew up a line of battle in front of the wrecked bridge and engaged in a distracting exchange of fire that garnered the attention of the Confederates, leaving them oblivious to their impending doom.[306]

The saturation of unrelenting accuracy from the repeating arms fire resulted in the abandonment of the defenders' position and their solitary howitzer. The death knell came when a third battalion of the Eighth Tennessee under Major William Denton charged across the river, taking advantage of the shallow current below the bridge, and commenced rounding up the fleeing Confederates. While no accurate butcher bill was presented, it was noted that several Confederates were killed, fifty prisoners were taken and one howitzer was captured. Likewise, unsubstantiated Confederate reports make mention of several men cut down in Major Denton's command, whose bodies could be seen floating down the river and scattered around the wooded hillside that led to the crossing.[307]

Following their victory at Rocky Ford, the marauders entered Morganton with a ravenous appetite for destruction and peril. Local lore tells of Union men interrogating the local women of Morganton with cocked pistols strategically placed between their eyes in an effort to extract the locations of their valuables. As the disinclined emancipators rode into Morganton, racial tensions came full steam when one unidentified trooper improvised a morbid take on an old martial tune: "Hail Columbia happy land, if I don't shoot a nigger I'll be damned!" Following this boastful doggerel, the trooper drew his pistol and loosed a shot that downed a black camp follower, hence inaugurating a mad-dash panic of freedmen from the confines of the column under the leadership of a false Moses.[308]

As the column returned to the town proper, the command structure broke down. Whether Gillem moved to prevent the frenzy is lost to history; however, what is known is that every house in Morganton was preyed on by troopers who had no care for the protocol of behavior expected of disciplined soldiers. Every pound of food, intrinsic valuable and personal firearm was pilfered by the unruly command. Subsequent to the chronic ransacking, the undefended population nervously rested in worrisome pensiveness, wondering if the locusts would return.[309]

Along with the ailments inflicted on the town, the surrounding areas were assaulted. A local sawmill owner was helpless to watch as the raiders burned his mill and barn and confiscated his livestock in the name of reuniting the South with the remainder of the Union. Before they were surrendered, the mill owner, John H. Pearson, hid his mules and mounts in secluded groves on his property. Holding Pearson at gunpoint, the troopers demanded of the women inside his home that the beasts of burden be produced or their patriarch would meet his demise and the property burned. After much heartache, the women capitulated, and crisis was averted with the heartbreaking sight of the last of their four-legged property disappearing over the horizon in tow behind the smirking troopers.[310]

At the height of the pillage of Morganton, spirits were uncovered, and their free flow led to unavoidable repercussions. While countless homes were plundered at the hands of intoxicated soldiers, the tragedy that unfolded at R.C. Pearson's home was of notable disturbance. On the same night that Gillem's men reentered the town, inebriated soldiers forced entry into the house and ransacked the residence of the commissioner of the Western North Carolina Railroad. The unadulterated thievery continued until a dutiful officer arrived and ordered the men to vacate the building after drawing his heavy revolver.[311]

At the point of a Colt, the frustrated burglars withdrew from their bountiful horde. Following their exit, the lieutenant posted a guard. However, the guards were not as concerned with the Pearson household as they were personal comfort and abandoned their position. Following their vacation, the Pearson household was visited by camp followers from the mountains and renegade blacks who made short order of whatever valuables remained inside the house following the gallivanting of the troopers. After the house was stripped of clothing, carpets, linens, curtains and silverware, the family was left in a stark-naked room, huddled in shock.[312]

The privations bestowed on the town of Morganton were only the beginning. Following the exit of Stoneman from the scene, the raid took on ominous tones of opportunism, revenge and class warfare. The scoundrels who would cement the raid's reputation in infamy were not the Union men from above the Mason-Dixon line but the "Home Yankees" from the anti-secessionist mountains who had for too long abided the abuses and excesses of luxury cherished by the cotton aristocracy. The raid now became the living embodiment of the envy and angst the mountaineers had long held against their lowland counterparts, and hell was to follow the cronies of Gillem.

"The Sympathy We Used to Feel for the Loyal Tennesseans Is Being Rapidly Transferred to Their Enemy"

G et the Hell out of my way, buck face!" The piercing squall of the dirt-stained, middle-aged woman was only intensified by the sharp whistle created by the periodic absence of strategic teeth. The insult, tantamount to the verbal castration that being branded a cuckold imparts, had its desired effect, as the stunned trooper parted with his prime real estate within the confines of the doorway, opening a wide path through which the diminutive firebrand could pass. With a cursory sideways scowl as the only acknowledgement of her triumph in the contest of wills and her newfound status as alpha of the group, the narrow-framed hellion entered the home of R.C. Pearson. Surveying the foyer for any sign of wealth, the sandy-haired woman, still sporting a grease-stained and charred apron pinned to her tattered day dress, rounded the corner into the sitting room. Freezing midstride, she was greeted upon entry by an unexpected scene: seven troopers from the rearguard detail stood in half-engaged observation, while an eighth threatened the matron of the Pearson family with revolver in hand as tears of petrified fear streamed from her eyes.[313]

Paying little heed to the dilemma of Mrs. Pearson, the Appalachian scamp who had a hip-high smudged-face in tow was followed into the ornate house by another two dozen eyes flush with the same hunger that resided in hers. The bulging haversacks of the nine blue-clad antagonists was all the indication needed for the woman to come to the conclusion that anything of direct monetary value had already been lifted from the premises. Locking eyes with lace curtains that were hanging directly behind the detained matron of the house, only a moment of hesitation passed before the unnamed camp follower walked toward the window and commenced to harvest the delicate cloth from its rod. The action of the mother and vain efforts by her child to emulate the diabolical actions of her parent were license enough for the rest of the unkempt cavalcade to dissect the Pearson holdings.[314]

Surging back from a state of shock to the unfortunate reality of her situation, Mrs. Pearson was riveted by the scene that was unfolding. Not resigned to watch the carefully planned aesthetic that was her sitting room demolished and pocketed before her eyes, the besieged socialite spoke up with adamancy similar to that of a mother protecting her offspring. "Take your hands off it all! Put it back, so help me God if you don't put it all back." Expending little more than a momentary glance at the glowering face, filled with hate at the insolence of her social inferiors directly disregarding a direct command, the women of the South Mountains continued to harvest her economic windfall.

"You ignorant heathens, goddamn your eyes, I told you to put it all back!" The scream at the top of her lungs was now drawing the amusement of her armed captors. "You ignorant unwashed whores—put it back!" The brashly condescending commands garnered the attention of the alpha female, who sprung at her prey with the lightning-quick ferocity of a copperhead ambushing an unsuspecting traveler stepping over deadfall. "Who in the hell do you think you are to curse me in front of my goddamn young'n?" The perplexity of the socialite's trespass was evident in the confounding contradiction of the counter insult.

In no time, the sitting room was void of any semblance of luxury; the only traces of its former decorative glory were the bulging croker sacks bursting at their interlocking burlap weaves with the afternoon's opportunistic gorging. Taking their cue from the Appalachian spitfire, many of the coconspirators began to openly heckle the matriarch, a trespass that transformed the offended, as her body began to quiver with intense nausea created by the combination of helplessness and an uncontrollable surge of adrenaline. Overcome with a multitude of emotions, the intense tremble finally toppled her senses, and Mrs. Pearson glaringly expelled what little protest remained inside her body as she hurled woeful titles at the mob, condemnations that ranged from assaults against their literacy and personal hygiene to accusations of belligerence in their faithful observance of whatever cussed deity, if any, they owed allegiance.[315]

While the performance was of the utmost amusement to the nine troopers who cast late-afternoon shadows on the far walls of the room, in which many of the dark specters danced doubled over in sidesplitting delight, the diligent scavengers soon grew weary as the spectacle lost all allure. Taking cues from the dismissive marauders nearest to the doorway leading to the adjoining room, the soiled rabble began to migrate into other unexplored areas of the house. Simultaneously assaulting the dining room and kitchen, sounds of drawers being shucked from the various hutches that inhabited the rooms were periodically interrupted by the sound of shattering china. While the easily malleable silverware, which lent itself to reduction into ingots with minimal effort, had long since made it into the hands of the amused troopers, the muted clang of cast iron being carefully situated into sacks indicated that this later wave of bandits was taking steps to cart off her crockery and cookware.[316]

Knowing full well that the tempest of pillage was unstoppable, Pearson's head sunk toward her chest as the remorseful regret of true helplessness began to take hold. In a moment of true abandon, the aging socialite attempted to reason with the absent shepherd, who was allowing this tribulation to unfold before her tear-reddened eyes. With the trudging vibration indicative of the swinish multitude's adventure to the upper floors of her violated sanctuary, it was clear that her pleas with the Almighty were an exercise in silent futility. Although forsaken to her own fate by divine apathy, she still hung to one final string of hope: the wily nature of a forgotten Morganton carpenter who had built her dwelling complete with a strategically hidden closet in the master bedroom.[317]

Apprehensively counting the steps, Mrs. Pearson predicted the order that the rooms of her inner sanctum were sullied with tragic accuracy. Images of the grubby hands of the Appalachian heathens greedily pawing away at her raiment, in some instances shredding the fine garments as lustful scuffles broke out amongst the vultures, stoked the embers of rage that had begun to subside. A well-timed hack in the throat of an inattentive trooper was enough to remind her of the quandary and that she was ultimately helpless to disrupt the sacking.

It was there in a disheveled master bedroom that the party—now completely stocked with what they saw as their just rewards from years of gleaning the bottom of the barrel for any scraps of fair treatment in the marketplace that happened to fall from the greedily wasteful banquet of the planter class—that the mob of Appalachian dowagers began the slow exit of the home. For a moment, it appeared as if the deity had shown a semblance of favor toward the besieged socialite. In the flicker of an overly observant eye, however, the same sandy-haired banshee who had confronted her supposed social better with the pent-up ferocity of a long-beaten dog noticed an anomaly—an out-of-place interruption in the bead board that was partially concealed by an oddly placed chest of drawers. Upon further inspection, it was clear that the distinctive crease was, in fact, a skillfully disguised hinge for a hidden doorway. As a wave of voracious telepathy rolled through the lustful hens, it became clearly evident to all that a treasure-trove had been unearthed.

In short order, one of the inquisitive looters returned with a broad-faced axe procured from a nearby outbuilding. Ignoring all the benefits offered by a strategic evaluation of her target, the fortune hungry jackal plunged the narrow edge of the implement blindly into the wall without yielding as much as an inch of penetration for her efforts. Exerting a grunt as the pitted iron blade was extracted from its newfound home, the struggling laborer tensed her muscles in an effort to exert more force in her next attempt. Although the second malevolent rap against the obstruction that hid the unseen trove bore similar effects, subsequent efforts made progress as the door began to cave in as it was reduced to haggard bits.[318]

Haunted by the repetitive thuds that signified the destructive nature of the events transpiring outside her view, Pearson could only lament the insulting nature of the final misfortune that was about to unfold. As the reverberation of each impact rattled the floor joist directly overhead, the silent sufferer could only count the moments until her last remaining virgin stash was despoiled. Fraught with anticipation, her estimation on the arrival of the moment of truth did not disappoint. Echoing throughout the vacant chambers of the vandalized abode, the high-pitched yelps of elation broke loose, leaving no doubt that the fate of her remaining provisions was sealed.

It was there, in the ruined confines of the boudoir, that tragedy collided headlong with gallows humor. Shearing the closet of its sequestered valuables, the pariahs were delighted with the collection of currency, foodstuffs and libations that were extracted from the niche. As the goods followed the bucket brigade of light fingers, an item of particular interest surfaced. Tucked toward the far corner of the cavity was a basket laden with approximately four bottles of aged champagne that the Pearson family had held in their cellar over the years.[319]

New wine, a sparkling concoction that had surely never traversed the lips of its newfound owners, was a high-value prize that was met with careful evaluation to determine with whom the windfall should reside. Silently standing in the corner of the room, yet studious in her plunder, was an ancient granny, whose eyes were transfixed on the seductively curved green bottles. The decision was seemingly preordained, as the weathered, yet strong, hands of the Appalachian practitioner were respectfully entrusted with one of the pinched bottles. Grasping the emerald idol in her hands, twinkling eyes saturated with pride at the pristine possession, the elderly bandit did not say a solitary word; that is, until the first cork was loosed from its seat.[320]

The violent eruption of the sparkling fermentation was all the alarm needed to unnerve one of its liberators, a woman of middle age who instantly let the three-quarter-filled vestal plummet to the floor out of unexpected shock. Bolting from the room in a state of panic, the bewildered mob followed her progression out of the room and down the stairs with unbridled curiosity. Of the horde, none was heeding the panicky reaction of the previously beguiled with a deeper, worried fascination than that of the befuddled granny. Casting a disbelieving eye at her suspicious windfall, doubt ran rampant through her geriatric mind.[321]

Striking her mind with the obviousness of a thunderbolt, the elder of the band came to the only logical conclusion: "That damned spirit is pizen!" In a vain effort to state the obvious to her unlettered collogues, she said, "I have never seen pop skull bark in such a manner. That mistress snuck it in there to upend us." Hesitation, for a brief moment, filled the room before the rudiments of reason overtook the ill-founded speculation that was spreading through the population. With a multitude of eyes wide at the protesting herbalist, who at this point had softly surrendered the bottle to the floor in a cautious effort not to rupture open the toxic ambrosia, the mob was in a suspended state of disbelief at their senior-most member's reaction to the flight of the spongy projectile.[322]

Entering the room with the heavy steps customary of mounted footwear, one of the rearguards arrived just in time to be welcomed with the sight of the panicky woman and the plethora of dumbfounded faces. It took no time for the Appalachian trooper to ascertain where the dilemma had originated. While not raised in the lap of East Tennessee luxury, his forays over the previous two years had not left his tongue ignorant of the dry sweetness of the French pleasantry. Borrowing the limitedly partaken bottle that was previously dropped to the floor in a mad panic, the trooper upended the dusty decanter and took a deep swig.[323]

Although an exercise in cordial instruction, the refreshing lesson was entirely ignored by the distraught apothecary, who was mortally swayed in the merits of her convictions. Dismissing her curse-filled departure from the room with a heartfelt chuckle, the trooper soon followed with a slyly lifted bottle of romantic ambrosia that had changed ownership three times in as many minutes. Shortly after the departure of the bedroom's colorful inhabitants, the rabble began to trickle downstairs and eventually out the front door. After a final survey of the residence for any trace of value that may have been ignored by the voracious autopsy, the rearguard departed the Pearson home. There, in the early evening dark, Mrs. R.C. Pearson sat with head in hands, shedding what little emotion she still possessed through swollen tear ducts.

The events that transpired at the Pearson home in the late afternoon hours of April 18 were a sobering omen of what was to come. Although the raid still bore the imprint of his surname, a specter that still haunts the folk traditions of Southern Appalachia to this very day, George Stoneman's departure from his charge heralded a new phase in the exhaustive adventure that had been evolving since the final week of March. In spite of the countless hundreds of thousands of dollars' worth of government and private property destruction that the column had accomplished, the worst privations were still to come.

Striking out for Asheville on the morning of the eighteenth, the newly independent Alvan Gillem set his sights on accomplishing a final conclusion to the heartbreaking conflict that had devastated his beloved mountain region. Likewise, loyalist officers, such as John Miller, were determined not to spend the remainder of their lives subjecting their families to periodic retribution at the hands of unreconstructed secessionist mountaineers, for lack of better words. The war in Southern Appalachia was to be decided at this moment. Then there were the enlisted men from both sides of the mountains, still saturated with hate from the injuries their families had suffered at the hands of their rebellious neighbors. With all the wrathful hallmarks of the blood feud, compounded with the idea that the unchecked pillage that many of the impoverished enlisted men were using to improve their station was at an end, the "Home Yankees" and the division's commander set out for the crest of the Blue Ridge with new objectives in mind: opportunistic warfare and revenge. Intermixed with political events that were unfolding unbeknownst to them, their adventure was about to experience a watershed moment.

Although the ride was far from complete, its strategic value to the Union war effort was at an end. In regards to the grand scheme that was lofted at its inception, the raid was a lukewarm success due to external events that had no bearing on the campaign once it was underway. Constant delays and the progression of Sherman into North Carolina before Stoneman could strike at his original target, the upstate of South Carolina, relegated the mounted demonstration to little more than an auxiliary measure. Given its limited scope in the greater theme of Sherman's invasion of the Carolinas and its multitude of aborted starts, the troopers who funneled across the Blue Ridge were impressively efficient in the execution of their orders, thus ultimately transforming the raid from an inconsequential side venture into a resounding tactical success. Although Stoneman narrowly avoided career assassination by undertaking even the most trivial token of a late start, once underway, the raid was explosive in damage, and its logistical impact in the closing weeks of the conflict was widely acknowledged by many of Stoneman's contemporaries.

Beginning with his late-March entry into Western North Carolina by way of Boone, Stoneman's tenure along the Appalachian rim was disastrous for these virgin lands of the Confederacy. Partly due to a blessing in disguise that arrived in the form of inclement weather, the column's failure to cross at predetermined fords along the Yadkin left the Confederate defenders of the region scratching their heads as to their ultimate destination, generating an anxious confusion that greatly hampered a proper defense of the region, as soldiers were transferred from location to location in an effort to defend against straw men. Riding along an east-by-northeastern route, the troopers inflicted a level of damage to a weathered Confederate infrastructure in North Carolina that was total—mischief that not only impeded the movement of supplies throughout the region but also harkened an ominous warning of what was to come in southwestern Virginia and, later, the North Carolina Piedmont.

While the definition of the raid was still evolving in the last weeks of April 1865, its impact on the Army of Northern Virginia's hopes of sustaining itself in rural southwestern Virginia was evident with the benefit of hindsight. Descending on the uninterrupted infrastructure scattered along the east slope of the Blue Ridge like rampant locusts, the demolishers uprooted no fewer than one hundred miles of track in two states, razed no fewer than a half dozen arms depositories to the ground, directly interrupted munitions and war goods in transit and left a temporary occupying presence in many key boroughs that were strategic to Lee's retreat from the Petersburg salient. The destruction of the utmost significance was the annihilation of many key bridges and trestles; due to the lack of manpower and material, both became nearly impossible to replace in this late hour of the war. By the time Stoneman had left his men in the hands of Gillem, nearly two dozen of the spans had been rendered useless or outright destroyed. The end result, while immediately unbeknownst to the troopers under Stoneman, was that the various actions of the division around Lynchburg gave the illusion to a dying Confederate behemoth that it was surrounded—a perception of helplessness that led directly to its surrender.

On top of the infrastructure devastation, the damage to the dwindling stores of Rebel accoutrements was irreplaceable. Although the blockade had greatly hindered the flow of war goods into the Southern nation, the mother of invention had fostered a well-entrenched domestic production infrastructure that ran at full speed in the communities haunted by the raid. The wanton destruction of the thousands of uniforms, leather accoutrements, stands of arms, ammunition and incendiary shells rendered this heartfelt exercise in futility useless; in the end, what the Federal government could not deprive their tragic opponent on the high seas, they robbed from it by sending well-armed divisions against rearguard, invalidated defenders. After passing through the filtered lenses of collective memory, the tragedy of lopsided late-hour assaults against hearth and industry lay the foundations for the majority of future lore concerning the raid.

For generations to come, families would pass down stories of ill events that transpired on their ancestors' property. Tragedies, most of which were steeped in the truthful exaggeration of memory, lent themselves to a skillful amalgamation that simultaneously bred a sense of pride and victimization in the storytelling. To the everlasting regret of those hypnotized by the intoxicating allure of oral history, the emergence of "Lost Cause" mythology in the postwar South greatly purified the oral history of the war in Southern Appalachia.

Many of the tales originating from the raid's "Home Yankee" participants have faded from memory due to their conflict with the predominant culture. The end result was that these highly misunderstood patriots were left vilified in local folklore without necessary ammunition to defend themselves—yet another cultural victory for the former planter aristocracy. While it is impossible to truly measure the extent of the financial impact on the civilians unfortunate enough to lie in the path of the troopers, destruction and robbery were not the only components of the campaign.

Although the war was in its death throes, the possibility of an organized guerrilla movement developing in the mountains was very real. Even though the idea had been dismissed by Robert E. Lee, in spite of ambiguous snide comments to his subordinate officers that if the spry young men sought to bleed the land dry, then let them, the sporadic ambushing of Stoneman's command was evidence that the terrain afforded ambiguity for anyone who elected to continue the war one Minié ball at a time. It was with this fear in mind that the raiders' North Carolina efforts made an immediate contribution to the post-Appomattox conflict.[324]

With the destruction of the massive stockpile of war goods at Salisbury, the last functional arsenal in the region was reduced to cinders—an event that retarded the further efforts of the Army of Tennessee should it have elected to maintain its position in the field. Although the greater teeth of a Confederate lion were withdrawn with much hardship, it was the day-to-day destruction of Confederate rail infrastructure and the large Union presence in the region that made any attempt to effectively assemble a collection of underground fighters outside the most isolated coves of Southern Appalachia an exercise in futility. Weary of the potential for a budding guerrilla movement, it was the original intention of the high command to entrench fragments of the division in strategic positions following their exit from Salisbury in an effort to dissuade the local population from beginning to attempt such a murderous undertaking. In the end, the efforts were pointless, as a defeated South had lost the majority of its appetite for futile bloodshed.

Even though Ulysses S. Grant later acknowledged, much to his gut-churning lament, that the Stoneman Raid was a success of limited scope for the Union war effort, as it existed in April 1865, a monumental change was on the horizon. What followed was a failure of catastrophic proportions, largely due to the breakdown of command and the dereliction of duty. As the command left Morganton bound for the soon-to-be-discovered martial obstruction at Swannanoa Gap, a paradigm shift occurred. Although service to the Union was the glue that held the two halves together—legitimate protectors of *Columbia* and rightfully vindictive "Home Yankees"—the raid soon deteriorated into two factions: those who still abandoned their advantageous looting long enough to maintain the order of the day versus those who had reverted back to their clannish states and had opted to explore self-emancipation against the planter aristocracy.

The weeks that were to follow the Stoneman—now Gillman—Raid became monumental pillars for the folk culture of the Appalachian rim of North Carolina, the counties that composed the foothills of South Carolina and the rolling plains of central Georgia. Seemingly everywhere at once, tradition holds that the lecherous riders who halfheartedly attached themselves to the invading column imposed their will on the pious generations of the upland South at gunpoint. While local lore juxtaposes sympathy toward those who had their life savings carted off by the Appalachian loyalists, the reality of events was that the men who engaged in opportunistic looting were doing less damage to the status quo of the antebellum South than had been rendered on them by their supposed prewar social betters. While the war was nowhere the social realignment that many twentieth-century contests would become, the hostilities in Western North Carolina and the upstate of South Carolina were conducted in a theater flush with ripe targets that only the apologetic Southern nationalist of the ensuing decades would dismiss as honest-to-God victims of the rampage undertaken at the hands of their impoverished and unwashed regional neighbors.

Regardless of the debate that revolved around the true intentions of the "Home Yankees," the intrusion of the column into the unsuspecting counties of the South was advantageous for the war effort, as it left the relatively unburdened with a distaste of war in their mouth that would not soon expire. Although the reinvention of the Stoneman Raid was wrought with mild benefits to the Union war effort, the end result for the local population was utter catastrophe. While the command traversed more ground than any other mounted expedition, roughly six hundred miles by the time the column reached Statesville, the actions taken in the final weeks of the adventure could be perceived as unforgivable in the minds of all but the most extreme military strategist.[325]

It was at this point that the raiders' mission took an unexpected turn. With the arrival of word that Confederate president Jefferson Davis was on the lam, the men of Gillem's division were selected to block the escape of the Confederate cabinet along the border of the two Carolinas and, if need be, follow the renegade leader to the "ends of the Earth." War, an unfortunate human habit that brings out the worst in all men, is conducted with a degree of decorum, no matter how sadistic the nature of its participants. The thrill of the hunt, steeped in the primal satisfaction that stirs the loins with the erotic desire of bloodlust, had a transformative effect on the nature of the raid. In the end, of the many factors that led to the disintegration of discipline and rampant civilian hardships that were to follow the command's departure from Statesville, only the frenzy of sadistic elation that was generated from the hunt for the Rebel leader lent itself as a paradigm for the overt debauchery that was to signify the last few weeks of April and the majority of May 1865.[326]

Although discipline was rapidly collapsing division-wide, two separate manifestations of violence and devastation that sported the moniker "Stoneman Raid" were ultimately polar opposites in the delivery of their destruction. While the organized devastation was advantageous to the Union war efforts in Virginia and North Carolina in the closing weeks of April 1865, what followed was an exercise in quasi-organized hell raising. A studious observer of history would be hard-pressed to find another cadre of regular soldiers who donned the indigo-saturated wool of the Union as ravenous in their lack of discipline, dereliction of duty and conduct of class warfare in the name of social realignment as the riders who accompanied Alvan Gillem into the western extremes of the Carolinas and central Georgia. While divorced from the column that ventured out of Morganton physically, George Stoneman's name would live on in infamy for the events that followed the afternoon of April 18, 1865.

Notes

INTRODUCTION

1. Oliver, *Faithful Heart*, 67; Keys, "Federal Pillage of Anderson," 80–86; Caroline R. Ravenel to Isabella Middleton Smith, May 18, 1865 in Smith, Smith and Childs, *Manson Smith Family Letters*, 213.
2. Ibid.
3. Ibid.
4. Ibid.
5. Ibid.
6. Ibid.
7. Ibid.
8. Ibid.
9. Ibid.
10. Ibid.
11. Ibid.
12. Ibid.
13. Ibid.
14. Van Noppen, *Stoneman's Last Raid*, 11.
15. For further study of the raid, the 1961 efforts of Dr. Ina Woestemeyer Van Noppen are unsurpassed. While Dr. Van Noppen's work concentrates heavily on events of the raid pertaining to North Carolina and largely ignores participants below the rank of general, her work is still largely referenced by historians of the raid with due merit.

Chapter 1

16. Fordney, *George Stoneman*, 33–34; Price, *Across the Continent*, 97–98.
17. Ibid.
18. Ibid.
19. Fordney, *Stoneman at Chancellorsville*, 8.
20. Fordney, *George Stoneman*, 8–9.
21. Ibid., 11–13.
22. Ibid., 13–14.
23. Ibid., 15–17.
24. Ibid., 15–19, 22; Roberts, *Mormon Battalion*, 38. For further information on the trials and tribulations of the Mormon Battalion and its march westward, see Tyler, *Concise History*.
25. Fordney, *George Stoneman*, 23–24; Tyler, *Concise History*, 239–40; Roberts, *Mormon Battalion*, 43.
26. Fordney, *George Stoneman*, 28–29.
27. Ibid., 32; Price, *Across the Continent*, 87.
28. Fordney, *George Stoneman*, 33–34; *War of Rebellion*, series I, vol.1, 579.
29. Ibid.
30. Fordney, *George Stoneman*, 33–34; *War of Rebellion*, series I, vol.1, 579; Price, *Across the Continent*, 97.
31. Fordney, *George Stoneman*, 35; *War of Rebellion*, series I, vol. 2, 40.
32. Fordney, *George Stoneman*, 35–37; Sears, *George B. McClellan*, 72.
33. Fordney, *George Stoneman*, 37–38, Sears, *George B. McClellan*, 25, 72.
34. Fordney, *George Stoneman*, 44–47; Averill, "With the Cavalry," 430.
35. Fordney, *George Stoneman*, 46–47.
36. Ibid., 2–3, 5; *War of Rebellion*, series I, vol. 25, pt. 2, 111.
37. Fordney, *Stoneman at Chancellorsville*, 11–12; *War of Rebellion*, series I, vol. 25, pt. 1, 1066.
38. Ibid.
39. Fordney, *Stoneman at Chancellorsville*, 14–15; Longacre, *Mounted Raids*, 152–53, 157–59; *War of Rebellion*, series I, vol. 25, pt. 1, 1058.
40. Ibid.
41. Black, *Cavalry Raids*, 95–100; Starr, *Union Cavalry*, vol. 1, 360; Woodward, *Chestnut's Civil War*, 425, 453; Fordney, *Stoneman at Chancellorsville*, 16–19, 33, 42–46; Fordney, *George Stoneman*, 78; Longacre, *Mounted Raids*, 154–57, 173; *War of the Rebellion*, series I, vol. 25, pt. 2, 463.
42. Fordney, *Stoneman at Chancellorsville*, 47–54; Fordney, *George Stoneman*, 79–80; Longacre, *Mounted Raids*, 173.
43. Starr, *Union Cavalry*, vol. 1, 360; Fordney, *Stoneman at Chancellorsville*, 58–59; Fordney, *George Stoneman*, 84; *War of Rebellion*, series 3, vol. 3, 580.

44. Fordney, *George Stoneman*, 84–87; *War of Rebellion*, series I, vol. 32, pt.3, 269, 302, 361, 399, 500, 512.
45. Starr, *Union Cavalry*, vol. 3, 452; Fordney, *Stoneman Stoneman at Chancellorsville*, 40; Fordney, *George Stoneman*, 86–90; *War of Rebellion*, series I, vol. 38, pt. 4, 507; series I, vol. 38, pt. 2, 915.
46. Watkins, *Co. Aytch*, 199–200; Mathews, *McCook-Stoneman Raid*, 53, 121, 123-128; Dyer, *Fighting Joe Wheeler*, 183–86; Fordney, *George Stoneman*, 90–97; Black, *Cavalry Raids*, 180–82; Starr, *Union Cavalry*, vol. 3, 451, 453, 455, 461–69, 762–63; *War of Rebellion*, series I, vol. 38, pt. 2, 507, 762, 774, 804, 913–15, 917, 920.
47. Fordney, *George Stoneman*, 90–97; Mathews, *McCook-Stoneman Raid*, 53, 121, 123–28; Black, *Cavalry Raids*, 180–82.
48. Fordney, *George Stoneman*, 99–100; *War of Rebellion*, series I, vol. 38, pt.2, 914; series II, vol.7, 616–17.
49. Fordney, *George Stoneman*, 102–05; *War of Rebellion*, series I, vol. 39, pt.1, 554; vol. 45, pt. 2, 54, 59, 402; vol. 49, pt. 1, 616.
50. Fordney, *George Stoneman*, 102–05; Mays, *Saltville Massacre*, 13, 63–67, 69.
51 Ibid.

CHAPTER 2

52. Kirk, *Fifteenth Pennsylvania*, 493, 520–22; Van Noppen, *Stoneman's Raid*, 14–15; *War of Rebellion*, series I, vol. 49, pt. I, 330; Starr, *Union Cavalry*, vol. 3, 563; Trowbridge, "Stoneman Raid," 5; Fordney, *Stoneman's Raid*, 107.
53. U.S. Senate Committee, *Medal of Honor Recipients*.
54. Ibid.
55. Kirk, *Fifteenth Pennsylvania*, 493; *War of Rebellion*, series I, vol. 49, pt. 1, 408; Fordney, *Stoneman's Raid*, 106–07; Van Noppen, *Stoneman's Raid*, 7–9.
56. Ibid.
57. Kirk, *Fifteenth Pennsylvania*, 493; Fordney, *Stoneman's Raid*, 105–06; *War of Rebellion*, series I, vol. 45, pt. 2, 28, 402; vol. 49, pt. 1, 616, 663, 753, 810; Barrett, *North Carolina*, 93; Van Noppen, *Stoneman's Raid*, 6–7.
58. Ibid.
59. *War of Rebellion*, series I, vol. 49, pt. 1, 810.
60. Trowbridge, "Stoneman Raid," 5; Van Noppen, *Stoneman's Raid*, 8, 14–15; Kirk, *Fifteenth Pennsylvania*, 493, 520–22; *War of Rebellion*, series I, vol. 49, pt. 1, 330; Starr, *Union Cavalry*, vol. 3, 563; Fordney, *George Stoneman*, 107.
61. Ibid.
62. *War of Rebellion*, series I, vol. 49, pt. 1, 663.
63. Fordney, *George Stoneman*, 107; Starr, *Union Cavalry*, vol.3, 563; Trowbridge, "Stoneman Raid," 5.

64. Andres, *History of St. Clair County*, 670; *Detroit Evening News*, "A Brave Man—Some Anecdotes of the Late General S. B. Brown," March 18, 1893; Keys, "Federal Pillage of Anderson," 84.
65. *Knoxville Whig*, March 15, 1865; Historical Commission of Tennessee, *Tennesseans in Civil War*, vol. 1, 351–52; Scott and Angel, *Thirteenth Tennessee*, 112–13, 117, 138, 227, 255, 260; Graf and Haskins, *Papers of Andrew Johnson*, 540–42.
66. *War of Rebellion*, series I, vol. 49, pt. 1, 616; Key, "Federal Pillage of Anderson," 84; Black, *Cavalry Raids*, 185–86; Scott and Angel, *Thirteenth Tennessee*, 21–22, 263–64.
67. Kirk, *Fifteenth Pennsylvania*, 493.
68. Black, *Cavalry Raids*, 185; Mason, "Stoneman's Last Campaign," in *Sketches of War History*, vol. 3, 23.
69. Van Noppen, *Stoneman's Raid*, 9–10; Fordney, *George Stoneman*, 107–09; Kirk, *Fifteenth Pennsylvania*, 493.
70. Van Noppen, *Stoneman's Raid*, 10; *War of Rebellion*, series I, vol. 49, pt. 1, 330.
71. Ibid.; Kirk, *Fifteenth Pennsylvania*, 493.
72. Ibid.
73. Kirk, *Fifteenth Pennsylvania*, 493.
74. Dugger, *War Trails*, 204; Van Noppen, *Stoneman's Raid*, 16–18; Black, *Cavalry Raids*, 186; Kirk, *Fifteenth Pennsylvania*, 493.
75. Van Noppen, *Stoneman's Raid*, 16; Fordney, *George Stoneman*, 108; Black, *Cavalry Raids*, 186; Barrett, *Civil War in North Carolina*, 352; Dugger, *War Trails*, 204.
76. Van Noppen, *Stoneman's Raid*, 17; *War of Rebellion*, series I, vol. 49, pt. 2, 112; Fordney, *George Stoneman*, 108; Black, *Cavalry Raids*, 186; Barrett, *Civil War in North Carolina*, 352.
77. Van Noppen, *Stoneman's Raid*, 17.
78. Ibid.
79. Arthur, *History of Watauga County*, 178; Fordney, *George Stoneman*, 108; Van Noppen, *Stoneman's Raid*, 17; Black, *Cavalry Raids*, 181.
80. Spencer, *Last Ninety Days*, 193.
81. Van Noppen, *Stoneman's Raid*, 18.
82. Ibid.; Fordney, *George Stoneman*, 108.
83. *War of Rebellion*, series I, vol. 49, pt. 2, 112; Van Noppen, *Stoneman's Raid*, 18.
84. Van Noppen, *Stoneman's Raid*, 18.
85. Ibid., 19, 21.
86. Ibid., 20, 22.

Chapter 3

87. Van Noppen, *Stoneman's Raid*, 24.
88. Ibid.

89. Ibid.

90. Ibid.

91. Inscoe and McKinney, *Confederate Appalachia*, 246.

92. Van Noppen, *Stoneman's Raid*, 18, 24; Hickerson, *Echoes of Happy Valley*, 106–07; Barrett, *North Carolina*, 94; Van Noppen and Van Noppen, *Western North Carolina*, 10; Spencer, *Last Ninety Days*, 196–97; *War of Rebellion*, series I, vol. 49, pt. 1, 331.

93. Harper, *Reminiscences*, 45; Van Noppen, *Stoneman's Raid*, 25.

94. Kirk, *Fifteenth Pennsylvania*, 522–27; Van Noppen, *Stoneman's Raid*, 25–26.

95. Kirk, *Fifteenth Pennsylvania*, 522–27.

96. Ibid.

97. Ibid.

98. Kirk, *Fifteenth Pennsylvania*, 522–27; Van Noppen, *Stoneman's Raid*, 27–28.

99. Kirk, *Fifteenth Pennsylvania*, 522–27.

100. Ibid.

101. Trotter, *Bushwhackers*, 257–58; Kirk, *Fifteenth Pennsylvania*, 522–27; Van Noppen, *Stoneman's Raid*, 26.

102. Kirk, *Fifteenth Pennsylvania*, 522–27.

103. *War of Rebellion*, series I, vol. 49, pt. 1, 326–27.

104. Van Noppen, *Stoneman's Raid*, 29–30; Kirk, *Fifteenth Pennsylvania*, 520; Inscoe and McKinney, *Confederate Appalachia*, 247.

105. Inscoe and McKinney, *Confederate Appalachia*, 247; Van Noppen, *Stoneman's Raid*, 30–31; Kirk, *Fifteenth Pennsylvania*, 729.

106. Van Noppen, *Stoneman's Raid*, 31; Kirk, *Fifteenth Pennsylvania*, 494–95; *War of Rebellion*, series I, vol. 49, pt. 1, 327.

107. Van Noppen, *Stoneman's Raid*, 31–32; Kirk, *Fifteenth Pennsylvania*, 494.

108. Roman, *Military Operations*, vol. 2, 658–59; Barrett, *Civil War in North Carolina*, 356; Van Noppen, *Stoneman's Raid*, 60.

109. Kirk, *Fifteenth Pennsylvania*, 495; *War of Rebellion*, series I, vol. 49, pt. 1, 327–28; Van Noppen, *Stoneman's Raid*, 32.

110. Kirk, *Fifteenth Pennsylvania*, 495; Van Noppen, *Stoneman's Raid*, 33.

111. Hollingsworth, *History of Surry County*, 150; Kirk, *Fifteenth Pennsylvania*, 495; *War of Rebellion*, series I, vol. 49, pt. 1, 327–28.

112. Megargee, "Chang and Eng Bunker"; Wallace and Wallace, *The Two*, 248.

113. Ibid.

114. Kirk, *Fifteenth Pennsylvania*, 495; Van Noppen, *Stoneman's Raid*, 33.

115. Kirk, *Fifteenth Pennsylvania*, 495.

116. Van Noppen, *Stoneman's Raid*, 33.

117. Trowbridge, "Stoneman Raid," 34–35; Kirk, *Fifteenth Pennsylvania*, 495–96.

CHAPTER 4

118. Kirk, *Fifteenth Pennsylvania*, 496–97; Van Noppen, *Stoneman's Raid*, 34–35; Fordney, *George Stoneman*, 111–12; Trotter, *Bushwhackers*, 262.
119. Ibid.
120. Ibid.
121. Ibid.
122. Ibid.
123. Ibid.
124. Ibid.
125. Ibid.
126. Ibid.
127. Ibid.
128. Ibid.
129. Ibid.
130. Mason, *Sketches of War History*, 100; Kirk, *Fifteenth Pennsylvania*, 495; Van Noppen, *Stoneman's Raid*, 33; Trotter, *Bushwhackers*, 261–62; Barrett, *Civil War in North Carolina*, 353; Black, *Cavalry Raids*, 187.
131. *War of Rebellion*, series I, vol. 49, pt. 1, 331.
132. Ibid., 332; Van Noppen, *Stoneman's Raid*, 33–34.
133. Garren, *Mountain Myth*, 15–19; *War of Rebellion*, series I, vol. 49, pt. 1, 332; Van Noppen, *Stoneman's Raid*, 33–34.
134. Ibid.
135. Van Noppen makes note of the dispute over the outcome of the engagement in her work *Stoneman's Raid* by citing a letter from R.L. Beall to Cornelia Phillips Spencer, dated September 20, 1866.
136. *War of Rebellion*, series I, vol. 49, pt. 1, 332; Van Noppen, *Stoneman's Raid*, 33–34.
137. *War of Rebellion*, series I, vol. 49, pt. 1, 331; Kirk, *Fifteenth Pennsylvania*, 499.
138. Kirk, *Fifteenth Pennsylvania*, 496–97; Van Noppen, *Stoneman's Raid*, 34–35; Fordney, *George Stoneman*, 111–12; Trotter, *Bushwhackers*, 262.
139. Kirk, *Fifteenth Pennsylvania*, 496, 696; Van Noppen, *Stoneman's Raid*, 35.
140. Ibid.
141. Kirk, *Fifteenth Pennsylvania*, 496; Van Noppen, *Stoneman's Raid*, 35.
142. Ibid.
143. Kirk, *Fifteenth Pennsylvania*, 496.
144. Ibid.
145. Ibid.
146. Ibid.
147. Barrett, *Civil War in North Carolina*, 353; Kirk, *Fifteenth Pennsylvania*, 496; Van Noppen, *Stoneman's Raid*, 36.
148. Kirk, *Fifteenth Pennsylvania*, 496, 696; Van Noppen, *Stoneman's Raid*, 36.

149. Ibid.
150. Ibid.
151. Ibid.
152. Ibid.
153. Ibid.
154. Kirk, *Fifteenth Pennsylvania*, 496, 696.
155. *War of Rebellion*, series I, vol. 49, pt. 1, 332.
156. Ibid.
157. Morrill, *Two Carolinas*, 495; Van Noppen, *Stoneman's Raid*, 36.
158. *War of Rebellion*, series I, vol. 49, pt. 1, 332.
159. Ibid.; Barrett, *North Carolina*, 93.
160. Ibid.
161. Kirk, *Fifteenth Pennsylvania*, 500; *War of Rebellion*, series I, vol. 49, pt. 1, 332.
162. Barrett, *North Carolina*, 353.
163. Smith, *Lee and Grant*, 254–57; Coulter, *Confederate States of America*, 560; Bradley, *This Astounding Close*, 132; Foote, *Civil War Narrative*, 850–51; Early, *Memoir*, 137; Catton, *Grant Takes Command*, 454–55.

Chapter 5

164. *War of Rebellion*, series I, vol. 49, pt. 1, 332; Kirk, *Fifteenth Pennsylvania*, 500; Fordney, *George Stoneman*, 113.
165. Ibid.
166. Ibid.
167. Ibid.
168. Ibid.
169. Ibid.
170. Ibid.
171. Ibid.
172. Ibid.
173. Ibid.
174. Ibid.
175. *War of Rebellion*, series I, vol. 49, pt. 1, 332; Kirk, *Fifteenth Pennsylvania*, 500; Van Noppen, *Stoneman's Raid*, 37; Fordney, *George Stoneman*, 113.
176. Van Noppen, *Stoneman's Raid*, 37; Morill, *Two Carolinas*, 495; Barrett, *North Carolina*, 94; Barrett, *Civil War in North Carolina*, 353; Fordney, *George Stoneman*, 113; Trotter, *Bushwhackers*, 264.
177. Van Noppen, *Stoneman's Raid*, 37.
178. Ibid.
179. *War of Rebellion*, series I, vol. 49, pt. 1, 330; Kirk, *Fifteenth Pennsylvania*, 500; Van Noppen, *Stoneman's Raid*, 37–38; Morill, *Two Carolinas*, 495;

Barrett, *North Carolina*, 94; Barrett, *Civil War in North Carolina*, 353; Fordney, *George Stoneman*, 113; Trotter, *Bushwhackers*, 264.

180. *War of Rebellion*, series I, vol. 49, pt. 1, 330; Van Noppen, *Stoneman's Raid*, 37–38; Fordney, *George Stoneman*, 112.

181. Perry, *Free State of Patrick*, 164; Wilson, *Slaves in Wills*, 12–13, 41–43, 96; Patrick County Probate Records, Book 4, 103, 118, 148; Book 5, 279, 358.

182. Kirk, *Fifteenth Pennsylvania*, 538; Van Noppen, *Stoneman's Raid*, 39; Fordney, *George Stoneman*, 112; Morill, *Two Carolinas*, 495; Barrett, *North Carolina*, 94; Barrett, *Civil War in North Carolina*, 353; Trotter, *Bushwhackers*, 264.

183. Kirk, *Fifteenth Pennsylvania*, 538; Van Noppen, *Stoneman's Raid*, 39.

184. Ibid.

185. Ibid.

186. Ibid.

187. Ibid.

188. Fries, *Forsyth County*, 97; Kirk, *Fifteenth Pennsylvania*, 501; Van Noppen, *Stoneman's Raid*, 39; Fordney, *George Stoneman*, 112.

189. Ibid.

190. Kirk, *Fifteenth Pennsylvania*, 545; Clewell, *History of Wachovia*, 250; Van Noppen, *Stoneman's Raid*, 40–41.

191. Crews and Bailey, *Records of the Moravians*, 6562–63, 6589, 6601; Fordney, *George Stoneman*, 112; Van Noppen, *Stoneman's Raid*, 41.

192. Ibid.

193. Ibid.

194. Kirk, *Fifteenth Pennsylvania*, 501, 698–700; Van Noppen, *Stoneman's Raid*, 48–49.

195. Ibid.

196. Ibid.

197. Ibid.

198. Ibid.

199. Ibid.

200. Ibid.

201. Ibid.

202. Van Noppen, *Stoneman's Raid*, 43.

203. Crews and Bailey, *Records of the Moravians*, 6562–63.

204. Kirk, *Fifteenth Pennsylvania*, 501; Van Noppen, *Stoneman's Raid*, 44.

205. Kirk, *Fifteenth Pennsylvania*, 698.

206. Ibid.

207. Barrett, *Sherman's March*, 227; Davis, *Jefferson Davis*, 613–14; Johnson, *Pursuit*, 113–14; Kirk, *Fifteenth Pennsylvania*, 502.

208. Kirk, *Fifteenth Pennsylvania*, 502, 545–46.

209. Ibid.; U.S. Senate Committee, *Medal of Honor Recipients: 1863–1978*.

210. Ibid.

211. Kirk, *Fifteenth Pennsylvania*, 545–46.
212. Barrett, *Sherman's March*, 227; Davis, *Jefferson Davis*, 613–614; Johnson, *Pursuit*, 113–14; Kirk, *Fifteenth Pennsylvania*, 502, 545–46.
213. Crews and Bailey, *Records of the Moravians*, 6562–63, 6589, 6601; Van Noppen, *Stoneman's Raid*, 46.
214. Van Noppen, *Stoneman's Raid*, 46.
215. Fries, *Forsyth County*, 96; *War of Rebellion*, series I, vol. 49, pt. 1, 663.
216. *War of Rebellion*, series I, vol. 49, pt. 1, 333.
217. Ibid.; Van Noppen, *Stoneman's Raid*, 47.
218. Ibid.
219. Ibid.

CHAPTER 6

220. *War of Rebellion*, series I, vol. 49, pt. 1, 324, 333–34; Van Noppen, *Stoneman's Raid*, 62–63; Kirk, *Fifteenth Pennsylvania*, 504.
221. Ibid.
222. Ibid.
223. Ibid.
224. Ibid.
225. Ibid.
226. Roman, *Military Operations*, 646, 658; Van Noppen, *Stoneman's Raid*, 56–59; Crist, Rozek and Williams, *Papers of Jefferson Davis*, 419, 422-423.
227. Ibid.
228. Davis, *Jefferson Davis*, 614; Roman, *Military Operations*, vol. 2, 389–92; Fordney, *George Stoneman*, 113–14; Crist, Rozek and Williams, *Papers of Jefferson Davis*, 282.
229. Roman, *Military Operations*, 658–59; Van Noppen, *Stoneman's Raid*, 60–61; *Daily Carolina Watchman*, April 12, 1865; Fordney, *George Stoneman*, 113–14.
230. *War of Rebellion*, series I, vol. 49, pt. 1, 324, 333–34.
231. Kirk, *Fifteenth Pennsylvania*, 504; Van Noppen, *Stoneman's Raid*, 63–64; Fordney, *George Stoneman*, 113–14.
232. Van Noppen, *Stoneman's Raid*, 63–64; Fordney, *George Stoneman*, 113–14.
233. *War of Rebellion*, series I, vol. 49, pt. 1, 324, 333–34; Kirk, *Fifteenth Pennsylvania*, 504; Van Noppen, *Stoneman's Raid*, 63–64.
234. *War of Rebellion*, series I, vol. 49, pt. 1, 324, 333–34.
235. Bradshaw, *General Stoneman's Raid*; *War of Rebellion*, series I, vol. 49, pt. 1, 324, 333–34.
236. Bradshaw, *General Stoneman's Raid*; Van Noppen, *Stoneman's Raid*, 63–64; Fordney, *George Stoneman*, 113–14.

237. Van Noppen, *Stoneman's Raid*, 66.

238. Bradshaw, *General Stoneman's Raid*.

239. Ibid.

240. Ibid.

241. Ibid.; Van Noppen, *Stoneman's Raid*, 66.

242. Ibid.

243. Bradshaw, *General Stoneman's Raid*.

244. Van Noppen, *Stoneman's Raid*, 66.

245. Ibid.

246. Ibid.

247. Spencer, *Last Ninety Days*, 202.

248. Van Noppen, *Stoneman's Raid*, 68; Fordney, *George Stoneman*, 115–16.

249. Spencer, *Last Ninety Days*, 202; Fordney, *George Stoneman*, 115–16.

250. *War of Rebellion*, series I, vol. 49, pt. 1, 334; Van Noppen, *Stoneman's Raid*, 67; Fordney, *George Stoneman*, 114;

251. Ibid.

252 Kirk, *Fifteenth Pennsylvania*, 504; Henderson, "Salisbury Prison"; *Daily Carolina Watchman*, October 13, 1864; Van Noppen, *Stoneman's Raid*, 52–53.

253. Ibid.

254. Brown, "Prisoners Evacuated from Salisbury Just Before Stoneman Terror Came," *Salisbury Evening Post*, May 23, 1948; Van Noppen, *Stoneman's Raid*, 56–57.

255. Bushnog, *Stoneman Raid*, 5–6.

256. Bradshaw, *General Stoneman's Raid*; Spencer, *Last Ninety Days*, 202; Van Noppen, *Stoneman's Raid*, 68.

257. Ibid.

258. Durkin, *John Dooley*, 192; Bradshaw, *General Stoneman's Raid*; Van Noppen, *Stoneman's Raid*, 68;

259. Davis, *Jefferson Davis*, 614; Roman, *Military Operations*, vol. 2, 389–92; Johnson, *Jefferson Davis*, 114–15.

260. Durkin, *John Dooley*, 192; *War of Rebellion*, series I, vol. 49, pt. 1, 334; *Carolina Watchman*, April 16, 1866.

CHAPTER 7

261. Fordney, *George Stoneman*, 117.

262. Van Noppen, *Stoneman's Raid*, 69.

263. *Landmark*, December 1, 1887; Van Noppen, *Stoneman's Raid*, 69; Fordney, *George Stoneman*, 117–18.

264. Ibid.

265. Ibid.

266. *War of Rebellion*, series I, vol. 49, pt. 1, 324; Kirk, *Fifteenth Pennsylvania*, 505; *Landmark*, December 1, 1887; Van Noppen, *Stoneman's Raid*, 71.

267. Spencer, *Last Ninety Days*, 198; *War of Rebellion*, series I, vol. 49, pt. 1, 324; Van Noppen, *Stoneman's Raid*, 70.

268. Spencer, *Last Ninety Days*, 198; Van Noppen, *Stoneman's Raid*, 70.

269. Van Noppen, *Stoneman's Raid*, 70; Fordney, *George Stoneman*, 116.

270. Spencer, *Last Ninety Days*, 198; *War of Rebellion*, series I, vol. 49, pt.1, 324; Kirk, *Fifteenth Pennsylvania*, 504.

271. Kirk, *Fifteenth Pennsylvania*, 505; Van Noppen, *Stoneman's Raid*, 71–72; Fordney, *George Stoneman*, 117.

272. Van Noppen, *Stoneman's Raid*, 72; Fordney, *George Stoneman*, 116–17.

273. Kirk, *Fifteenth Pennsylvania*, 505; *Landmark*, December 1, 1877.

274. Ibid.

275. *Landmark*, December 1, 1877.

276. Ibid.

277. Kirk, *Fifteenth Pennsylvania*, 504; Woodward, *Chestnut's Civil War*, 778.

278. Kirk, *Fifteenth Pennsylvania*, 506.

279. Ibid.

280. Ibid.

281. Kirk, *Fifteenth Pennsylvania*, 507; Van Noppen, *Stoneman's Raid*, 73; Fordney, *George Stoneman*, 117.

282. Ibid.

283. Kirk, *Fifteenth Pennsylvania*, 505–07; Van Noppen, *Stoneman's Raid*, 73–74; Fordney, *George Stoneman*, 117.

284. Kirk, *Fifteenth Pennsylvania*, 505.

285. Ibid.

286. Ibid.

287. Kirk, *Fifteenth Pennsylvania*, 505; Van Noppen, *Stoneman's Raid*, 73–74; Fordney, *George Stoneman*, 117.

288. Kirk, *Fifteenth Pennsylvania*, 507.

289. Ibid.

290. Kirk, *Fifteenth Pennsylvania*, 507; Van Noppen, *Stoneman's Raid*, 74.

291. Ibid.

292. Van Noppen, *Stoneman's Raid*, 74.

293. *Landmark*, December 1, 1877.

294. Van Noppen, *Stoneman's Raid*, 75.

295. Ibid., 74.

296. Ibid., 75.

297. Ibid.

298. Ibid.

299. Ibid.

300. Kirk, *Fifteenth Pennsylvania*, 507.

301. Spencer, *Last Ninety Days*, 224; Van Noppen, *Stoneman's Raid*, 76.
302. Ibid.
303. Ibid.
304. Spencer, *Last Ninety Days*, 224; *War of Rebellion*, series I, vol. 49, pt. 1, 337; Van Noppen, *Stoneman's Raid*, 23–24.
305. *War of Rebellion*, series I, vol. 49, pt. 1, 335.
306. Ibid.
307. Ibid.
308. Van Noppen, *Stoneman's Raid*, 77.
309. Ibid., 78–80.
310. Ibid.
311. Ibid.
312. Ibid.

EPILOGUE

313. Van Noppen, *Stoneman's Raid*, 78.
314. Ibid.
315. Ibid.
316. Ibid.
317. Ibid.
318. Ibid.
319. Ibid.
320. Ibid.
321. Ibid.
322. Ibid.
323. Ibid.
324. Spencer, *Last Ninety Days*, 207–08; Freehling, *South vs. The South*, 197–98; McPherson, *Ordeal by Fire*, 519; Freeman, *Lee's Lieutenants*, 731, 738–39.
325. Thomas, Cowperthwait and Company, *A New Map of North Carolina with Its Canals, Roads, and Distances* (Philadelphia: Thomas, Cowperthwait and Company, 1850).
326. *War of Rebellion*, series I, vol. 49, pt. 1, 546–47.

Bibliography

Books

Anderson County, South Carolina: The Things that Made it Happen. N.p.: Anderson County Library, 1995.

Andreas, A.T. *History of St. Clair County, Michigan*. Chicago: A.T. Andreas & Company, 1883.

Arthur, John Preston. *A History of Watauga County, North Carolina*. Richmond, VA: Everett Waddey Company, 1915.

Barrett, John Gilchrist. *The Civil War in North Carolina*. Chapel Hill: University of North Carolina Press, 1963.

———. *North Carolina as a Civil War Battleground: 1861–1865*. Raleigh, NC: State Department of Archives and History, 1960.

———. *Sherman's March through the Carolinas*. Chapel Hill: University of North Carolina Press, 1956.

Black, Colonel Robert W. *Cavalry Raids of the Civil War*. Mechanicsburg, PA: Stackpole Books, 2004.

Blackwell, Joshua Beau. *Used to Be a Rough Place in Them Hills: Moonshine, the Dark Corner, and the New South*. Bloomington, IN: Author House Books, 2009.

Bradley, Mark L. *This Astounding Close: The Road to Bennett Place*. Chapel Hill: University of North Carolina Press, 2000.

Bradshaw, Harriet Ellis. *General Stoneman's Raid on Salisbury, North Carolina: A Reminiscence of April 12, 1865*. Chapel Hill: Southern Historical Collection, University of North Carolina, n.d.

Bushnog, William. *The Last Great Stoneman Raid*. Pamphlet from the Regimental Reunion of the Twelfth Ohio Cavalry, 1910.

Casstevens, Frances H. *The Civil War and Yadkin County, North Carolina: A History*. Jefferson, NC: McFarland & Company, Inc., Publishers, 1997.

Catton, Bruce. *Grant Takes Command*. New York: Little, Brown and Company, 1968.

Clewell, John Henry. *History of Wachovia in North Carolina: 1752–1902*. New York: Doubleday, Page and Company, 1902.

Coulter, Ellis Merton. *The Confederate States of America*. Baton Rouge: Louisiana State University Press, 1950.

Crews, C. Daniel, and Lisa D. Bailey, eds. *Records of the Moravians in North Carolina*. Vol. 12, *1856–1866*. Raleigh: Division of Archives and History, North Carolina Department of Cultural Resources, 2000.

Crist, Lynda Lasswell, Barbra J. Rozek and Kenneth H. Williams, eds. *The Papers of Jefferson Davis*. Vol. 11, *September 1864–May 1865*. Baton Rouge: Louisiana State University Press, 2004.

Davis, Burke. *The Long Surrender: A Brilliantly Realized, Panoramic History of the Collapse of the Confederacy and the Personal Ordeal of Its President, Jefferson Davis*. New York: Vintage Books, 1989.

Davis, William C. *Jefferson Davis: The Man and His Hour*. Baton Rouge: Louisiana State University Press, 2001.

Dugger, Shepherd M. *The War Trails of the Blue Ridge*. Banner Elk, NC: self-published, 1932.

Durkin, Joseph T., ed. *John Dooley, Confederate Soldier: His War Journal*. Washington, D.C.: Georgetown University Press, 1945.

Dyer, John P. *Fighting Joe Wheeler*. Baton Rouge: University of Louisiana Press, 1941.

Early, Jubal A. *A Memoir of the Last Year of the War of Independence in the Confederate States of America*. Columbia: University of South Carolina Press, 2001.

Foote, Shelby. *The Civil War, a Narrative: Red River to Appomattox*. New York: Random House, 1974.

Fordney, Ben Fuller. *George Stoneman: A Biography of the Union General*. Jefferson, NC: McFarland & Company, Inc., 2008.

———. *Stoneman at Chancellorsville: The Coming of Age of Union Cavalry*. Shippensburg, PA: White Mane Books, 1998.

Foster, Vernon. *Spartanburg: Facts, Reminiscences, and Folklore*. Spartanburg, SC: The Reprint Company, 1998.

Freehling, William W. *The South vs. The South: How Anti-Confederate Southerners Shaped the Course of the Civil War*. Oxford, UK: Oxford University Press, 2001.

Freeman, Douglas Southhall. *Lee's Lieutenants: A Study in Command*. Vol. 3. New York: Charles Scribner's Sons, 1944.

Fries, Adelaide. *Forsyth County*. Salem, NC: self-published, 1898.

Garren, Terrell T. *Mountain Myth: Unionism in Western North Carolina*. Spartanburg, SC: The Reprint Company, 2006.

Gordon, Larry. *The Last Confederate General: John C. Vaughn and His East Tennessee Cavalry*. Minneapolis, MN: Zenith Press, 2009.

Graf, Leroy P., and Ralph W. Haskins, eds. *The Papers of Andrew Johnson*. Vol. 7, *1864–1865*. Knoxville: University of Tennessee Press, 1986.

Greenville: Woven from the Past. Greenville, SC: Flour Daniel Corporation and the American Historical Press, 2000.

Hanna, A.J. *Flight into Oblivion*. Richmond, VA: Johnson Publishing Company, 1938.

Harper, G.W.F. *Reminiscences of Caldwell Count, North Carolina in the Great War of 1861–65*. Lenoir, NC: self-published, 1913.

Hickerson, Thomas Felix. *Echoes of Happy Valley: Letters and Diaries, Family Life in the South, Civil War History*. Chapel Hill: University of North Carolina Press, 1962.

Historical Commission of Tennessee. *Tennesseans in the Civil War*. Vol. 1. Knoxville: University of Tennessee Press, 1971.

A History of Tennessee from the Earliest Times to the Present, Together with an Historical and Biographical Sketch of Carter County. Nashville, TN: Godspeed Publishing Company, 1887.

Hollingsworth, J.C. *History of Surry County*. Greensboro, NC: W.H. Fisher Company, 1935.

Howard, James A. *Dark Corner Heritage*. Gowensville, SC: Greater Gowensville Association, 1980.

Huff, Archie Vernon. *Greenville: The History of the City and County in the South Carolina Piedmont*. Columbia: University of South Carolina Press, 1995.

Inscoe, John C., and Gordon B. McKinney. *The Heart of Confederate Appalachia: Western North Carolina in the Civil War*. Chapel Hill: University of North Carolina Press, 2000.

Johnson, Clint. *Jefferson Davis*. Secaucus, NJ: Citadel Press, 2008.

———. *Pursuit: The Chase, Capture, Persecution & Surprising Release of Confederate President*. N.p., n.d.

———. *Touring the Carolinas' Civil War Sites*. Winston-Salem, NC: John F. Blair Publisher, 1996.

Johnson, Robert Underwood, and Clarence Clough Buel, eds. *Battles and Leaders of the Civil War*. New York: The Century Company, 1887.

Kirk, Charles H., ed. *History of the Fifteenth Pennsylvania Volunteer Cavalry*. Philadelphia: Historical Committee of the Society of the Fifteenth Pennsylvania Cavalry, 1906.

Lattimore, Robin Spencer. *Across Two Centuries: The Lost World of Green River Plantation*. Rutherfordton, NC: Hilltop Publications, 2003.

Lawrence, James Walton, Sr. *The Shadows of Hogback*. Landrum, SC: The News Leader, 1979.

Longacre, Edward G. *Mounted Raids of the Civil War*. Lincoln: University of Nebraska Press, 1994.

Manigault, Arthur Middleton. *A Carolinian Goes to War: The Civil War Narrative of Arthur Middleton Manigault*. Edited by R. Lockwood Tower. Columbia: University of South Carolina Press, 1983.

Mason, Frank H. *Sketches of War History, Ohio Commandery of the Military Order of the Loyal Legion of the United States*. Cincinnati, OH: Robert Clarke, 1890.

Mathews, Byron H., Jr. *The McCook-Stoneman Raid*. Philadelphia: Dorrance & Company, 1976.

Mays, Thomas D. *The Saltville Massacre*. Abilene, TX: McWhiney Foundation Press of McMurry University, 1995.

McPherson, James M. *Ordeal by Fire: The Civil War and Reconstruction*. New York: McGraw-Hill Companies, 2001.

Morrill, Dan L. *The Civil War in the Two Carolinas*. Mount Pleasant, SC: The Nautical & Aviation Publishing Company of America, 2002.

Oliver, Robert, ed. *A Faithful Heart: The Journals of Emmala Reed, 1865 and 1866*. Columbia: University of South Carolina Press, 2004.

Otter, Richard C. *Anderson County: Twentieth Century Memories & Reflections*. Anderson, SC: Friends of the Library, 2004.

Perry, Thomas David. *The Free State of Patrick: Patrick County Virginia in the Civil War*. N.p.: Laurel Hill Publishing, 2005.

Price, George F. *Across the Continent with the Fifth Cavalry*. New York: D. Van Nostrand, 1883.

Recollections and Reminiscences: 1861–1865 through World War I. Vols. 3 & 7. N.p: South Carolina Division United Daughters of the Confederacy, 1992.

Richardson, James M. *History of Greenville County, South Carolina: Narrative and Biographical*. N.p.: Southern Historical Press, 1993.

Roberts, Brigham Henry. *The Mormon Battalion: Its History and Achievements*. Salt Lake City: The Desert News Press, 1919.

Roman, A. *The Military Operations of General Beauregard in the War Between the States, 1861–1865: Including a Brief Sketch and Narrative of Service in the War with Mexico*. Vol. 2. New York: Harper and Brothers, 1884.

Rowland, Dunbar, ed. *Encyclopedia of Mississippi History*. Vol. 2. Madison, WI: Selwyn A. Brant, 1907.

Scott, Samuel W., and Samuel P. Angel. *History of the Thirteenth Tennessee Volunteer Cavalry, U.S.A*. Johnson City, TN: Overmountian Press, 1987.

Sears, Stephen W. *George B. McClellan: The Young Napoleon*. New York: Ticknor and Fields, 1988.

Smith, Daniel E. Huger, Alice R. Smith and Arney R. Childs, eds. *Manson Smith Family Letters: 1860–1868*. Columbia: University of South Carolina Press, 1950.

Smith, Gene. *Lee and Grant: A Dual Biography*. New York: Meridian Printing, 1984.

Sondley, F.A. *A History of Buncombe County, North Carolina*. Spartanburg, SC: The Reprint Company, 1977.

Spencer, Cornelia Phillips. *The Last Ninety Days of the War in North Carolina*. Chapel Hill: University of North Carolina Electronic Publication, 2005.

Starr, Stephen Z. *The Union Cavalry in the Civil War*. 3 vols. Baton Rouge: Louisiana State University Press, 1979, 1981, 1985.

Stevenson, Mary, ed. *The Diary of Clarissa Adger Bowen, Ashtabula Plantation, 1865: with Excerpts from Other Family Diaries and Comments by Her Granddaughter, Clarissa Walton Taylor, and Many Other Accounts of the Pendleton Clemson Area, South Carolina, 1776–1865*. Pendleton, SC: Foundation for Historic Restoration in the Pendleton Area, 1973.

Swanson, James L. *Manhunt: The Twelve-Day Chase for Lincoln's Killer*. New York: Harper Collins Publishers, 2006.

Taylor, Mrs. Thomas, and Sallie Enders Conner, eds. *South Carolina Women in the Confederacy*. Columbia, SC: The State Company, 1903.

Thomas, Sam. *Jefferson Davis in South Carolina*. N.p: Palmetto Conservation Foundation, 1998.

Trotter, William R. *Bushwhackers: The Civil War in North Carolina, the Mountains*. Winston-Salem, NC: John F. Blair Publisher, 1988.

Tyler, Daniel. *A Concise History of the Mormon Battalion in the Mexican War, 1846–1847*. Salt Lake City, UT: self-published, 1881.

Vandiver, Louise Ayer. *Traditions and History of Anderson County*. Atlanta, GA: Ruralist Press, 1928.

Van Noppen, Ina Woestemeyer. *Stoneman's Last Raid*. Raleigh: North Carolina State College Press Shop, 1961.

Van Noppen, Ina Woestemeyer, and John J. Van Noppen. *Western North Carolina Since the Civil War*. Boone, NC: Appalachian Consortium Press, 1973.

Wallace, Irving, and Amy Wallace. *The Two: The Irresistibly Fascinating Story of the World's Most Famous Couple—The Original Siamese Twins*. New York: Bantam Books, 1979.

Watkins, Sam R. *Co. Aytch: A Side Show of the Big Show*. New York: Touchstone Books, 1997.

Wilson, Cynthia A. *Slaves in Wills, Inventories and Accounts in Patrick County Virginia, 1791–1864*. Seattle, WA: self-published, 2003.

Woodward, C. Vann, ed. *Mary Chestnut's Civil War*. New Haven, CT: Yale University Press, 1981.

Zuczek, Richard, ed. *Encyclopedia of the Reconstruction Era: Memphis Riot (1866)*. Westport, CT: Greenwood Press, 2006.

BIBLIOGRAPHY

ARTICLES

"Gen. William J. Palmer, A Builder of the West." *The World's Work: A History of Our Time* 25 (February 1908): 9898–9903.

Keys, Bland Thomas. "The Federal Pillage of Anderson, South Carolina: Brown's Raid." *South Carolina Historical Magazine* 76, no. 2 (Spring): 80–86.

Megargee, Louis N. "Chang and Eng Bunker." *Seen and Heard* (February 19, 1902).

Ryan, James G. "The Memphis Riots of 1866: Terror in a Black Community during Reconstruction." *Journal of Negro History* 62 (1977): 243–257.

Trowbridge, Brigadier General Luther S. "The Stoneman Raid of 1865." *Cavalry Journal* 24, no. 4. (Winter): 34–35.

GOVERNMENT DOCUMENTS

Patrick County Probate Records, Book 4 and Book 5. Patrick County, VA.

United States Senate Committee on Veterans' Affairs Report. *Medal of Honor Recipients: 1863–1978.* Washington, D.C.: Government Printing Office, 1979.

United States War Department. *The War of the Rebellion: A Compilation of the Official Records of the Union and Confederate Armies.* Washington, D.C.: Government Printing Office, 1880–1901.

NEWSPAPERS

Anderson Intelligencer (Anderson, SC)
Asheville Citizen-Times (Asheville, NC)
Carolina Spartan (Spartanburg, SC)
Charleston Daily Courier (Charleston, SC)
Daily Carolina Watchman (Salisbury, NC)
Detroit Evening News (Detroit, MI)
Edgefield Advisor (Edgefield, SC)
Knoxville Whig (Knoxville, TN)
Landmark (Statesville, NC)
Salisbury Evening Post (Salisbury, NC)
Spartanburg Journal (Spartanburg, SC)
Yorkville Enquirer (York, SC)

Index

About the Author

As a native of the upstate of South Carolina, Joshua Beau Blackwell has long been fascinated by the unsung struggles of the impoverished in Southern Appalachia and the upland South. While a student at the College of Charleston, Blackwell drew from his own experiences growing up in the working class of the region to build a foundation for careers in both the historical and educational fields. After graduating from the College of Charleston with a bachelor of arts in history, from the University of Charleston with a master of arts in history and from Converse College in Spartanburg, South Carolina, with a master of arts in teaching, Blackwell is presently employed as a high school teacher and adjunct history professor at two local colleges.

Visit us at
www.historypress.net